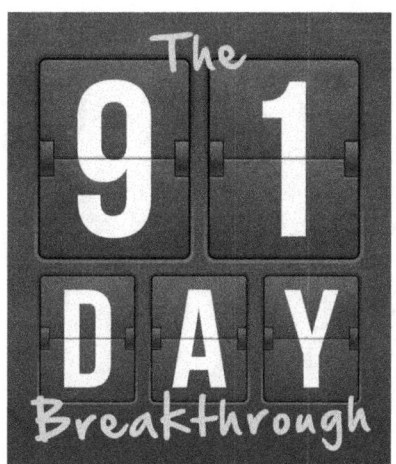

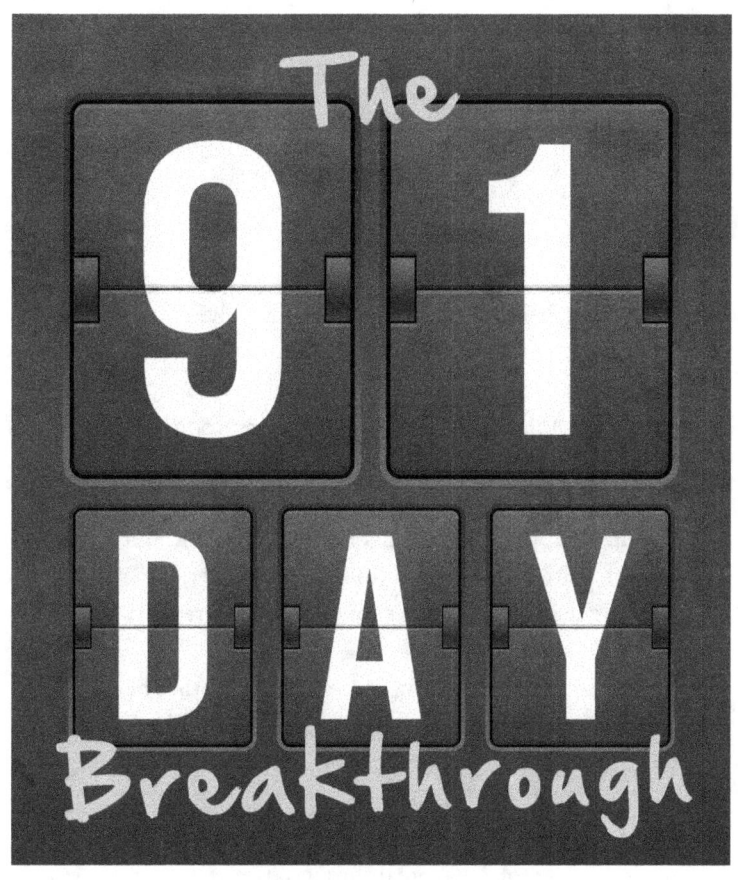

THE 91-DAY JOURNEY TO A NEW, BETTER YOU!

JOSEPH ABNEY

The 91 Day Breakthrough
Copyright 2016 by Joseph Abney/Innovative Products.
All rights reserved.

No part of this publication may be reproduced, stored in a retrieval system or transmitted, in any form or by any means—electronic, mechanical, photocopying, recording or otherwise—without prior written permission from the publisher, except for the inclusion of brief quotations in a review.

For information about this title or to order other books and/or electronic media, contact the publisher:
Innovative Products
P.O. Box 361
Farmington MO 63640
the91daybreakthrough.com

ISBN: 978-0-9975688-0-6 (print)
978-0-9975688-1-3 (eBook)

Printed in the United States of America

Foreword

Have you ever started an eating and exercise program, gotten good results in the first few weeks, and then given up?

You know what I am talking about. You're on a roll, feeling just a bit better, a few pounds dropped, and then temptation comes along.

That super-carb sugar bomb blows up your eating plan, or the planned workout got pushed out because of a work or family "emergency." Why did this happen? Simple. Really—your mindset had not changed. Long-term physical health is not about a diet and exercise plan—it's about a lifestyle mindset.

The 91 Day Breakthrough is all about mindset. It is the perfect guide to help you start your journey, change your mindset, and change your life.

I really do believe my quote, "What you feed your mind determines your appetite," is absolutely true—and this book is the ideal way to start changing your mind-set today and creating the healthy life you really want!

— Tom Ziglar, CEO, Ziglar, Inc.

Preface

This book is designed to be read one day at a time for the next 91 days. The goal is to motivate you to take the appropriate action daily that will bring you one step closer to your goals. By taking little steps on a daily basis, you will move ahead on your journey by leaps and bounds, and by doing so, by day 91 you will have become a new, better you. As you read this book on a daily basis, you should answer the questions at the end of each day and then immediately take action. Reading the book without taking the time to participate in the daily activities will move you only partly toward your goals. However, I believe if you truly commit for the next 91 days, all aspects of your life will improve, from career, health, and finances to your marriage and, ultimately, weight loss. Embrace the journey for the next 91 days, and you will be on the path to becoming the best you that you are designed to be.

Introduction

At the age of forty-three I woke up one day depressed, overweight, and feeling unfulfilled. It didn't happen overnight. Slowly but surely the life I was living was leading me to an early grave.

I wasn't planning my life. I was just existing. I ate the worst foods possible, and my weight kept creeping up. I traded what I wanted most for what I wanted right now, as so many of us do.

Then one day I decided my life had to change. As I started day 1, I weighed 256 pounds, just four pounds less than my heaviest. I resolved to make the changes I talk about in this book. These changes affected me positively, not just weight-wise but in all areas of my life. By the time I finished this book, my life had changed forever for the better.

I believe if you follow these same principles, your life will be changed, too. Will you join me on this journey for the next ninety-one days?

Table of Contents

INTRODUCTION ix

DAY 1: You Must Change If You Want Change 1

DAY 2: What Are You Waiting For? 5

DAY 3: The Millionaire 9

DAY 4: Stop the Madness 13

DAY 5: One Day at a Time 17

DAY 6: Food Is Not Your Friend 21

DAY 7: Slow and Steady 23

DAY 8: If You Slip, Don't Slide 25

DAY 9: Redeeming the Time 29

DAY 10: Be Like Mike 33

DAY 11: Know and Do 37

DAY 12: What Kind of Person Are You? 41

DAY 13:	Fail to Plan, Plan to Fail	45
DAY 14:	Don't Break	47
DAY 15:	The Mirror	49
DAY 16:	What's Your Excuse?	53
DAY 17:	Build a Puzzle	57
DAY 18:	Is It Worth It?	61
DAY 19:	Let It Erupt	65
DAY 20:	The Lifesaver	69
DAY 21:	Forming New Habits	73
DAY 22:	Step Up to the Plate	77
DAY 23:	Hope-Wish-Want	81
DAY 24:	Don't Fear	85
DAY 25:	What It Takes	87
DAY 26:	Hardest or Easiest	91
DAY 27:	Be Honest	95
DAY 28:	Holiday Time	97
DAY 29:	The Secret	101
DAY 30:	What's Eating You?	105
DAY 31:	Be Not Defined by a Number	109
DAY 32:	Victim or Victorious	111
DAY 33:	Are We Not Better?	115

Table of Contents

DAY 34:	Get Long-Term Vision	119
DAY 35:	Negative or Positive?	121
DAY 36:	Get Your Guard Up	125
DAY 37:	Fight for Your Right	127
DAY 38:	Concentrate on the Fundamentals	131
DAY 39:	Dig Deep	135
DAY 40:	Take Action	139
DAY 41:	Friend or Foe	143
DAY 42:	Smile Today	147
DAY 43:	Don't Quit Before Your Miracle	149
DAY 44:	Don't Wait	153
DAY 45:	A Day of Reflection	155
DAY 46:	Reward Yourself	167
DAY 47:	Mold Your Life	169
DAY 48:	Are You an Addict?	171
DAY 49:	Turn Some Pages	175
DAY 50:	Nothing New	177
DAY 51:	Move to Lose	181
DAY 52:	Make It Fun	185
DAY 53:	Accountability Partner	187
DAY 54:	2.3 Ounces	191

DAY 55:	You Are Where You Are	195
DAY 56:	The Reward	199
DAY 57:	Past Mistakes	203
DAY 58:	What's Right?	207
DAY 59:	Living Outside Your Comfort Zone	211
DAY 60:	Another Day of Reflection	215
DAY 61:	React or Respond?	221
DAY 62:	Self-Talk	225
DAY 63:	Self-Talk (Part 2)	231
DAY 64:	Path of Decision	233
DAY 65:	The A-Life	237
DAY 66:	Attitude of Gratitude	241
DAY 67:	Drained	245
DAY 68:	Determination of a Child	247
DAY 69:	Just Getting By	249
DAY 70:	Keep the Fire Burning	253
DAY 71:	Balance	257
DAY 72:	Loyalty	261
DAY 73:	What If	263
DAY 74:	Time	265
DAY 75:	Failure?	269

Table of Contents

DAY 76:	Breakthrough	273
DAY 77:	Partly or Fully Committed	275
DAY 78:	Lights, Camera, Action!	279
DAY 79:	Not Another Excuse	283
DAY 80:	Action Inspires	285
DAY 81:	Unleash Your Greatness	287
DAY 82:	Love Yourself	289
DAY 83:	Prepare	293
DAY 84:	Can-Do Attitude	295
DAY 85:	Learn	299
DAY 86:	More "What If"	301
DAY 87:	Body by You	303
DAY 88:	The Power of 2	305
DAY 89:	Self-Talk (Part 3)	309
DAY 90:	The Results	311
DAY 91:	A New Beginning	315
ACKNOWLEDGMENTS		317
ABOUT THE AUTHOR		319

You Must Change If You Want Change

You have just embarked on a journey that will change your life once and for all.

For the next ninety-one days we need to get clear about what has held us back in our life. Why we haven't take the weight off. Why we haven't advanced in our careers. Why we haven't seemed to overcome our addictions and depression. Perhaps our marriages and spiritual lives are suffering.

We all know that there are areas that need a little improving in our life. So why haven't we taken the appropriate actions to accomplish all we want in our life, and why do we let negative influence pull us down?

Life is short, and every day is precious. How much longer will we just wait for change? If we don't change now, when? You deserve your best life now! You already intuitively know what you should do for change! You just need a little spark to get yourself heading in the right direction.

This book is designed to get you heading in the direction in which you already know you should go. Whatever it is—whether it's advancing your career, working on a better marriage, growing spiritually, or getting your physical health under control—by day 91 you will improve by leaps and bounds.

By making minor, easily doable changes in your life in the next ninety-one days, you will see major improvements. You will became happier and healthier. You will break out of the slump that may have halted you in your career; at the same time you will grow in your relationships with family and friends.

I want you to view your life as a stream. If a stream stops flowing, what happens? It becomes stagnant. That's exactly where I was before I adopted the principles I talk about in this book. This may be exactly where you are, too.

What if you break out of your stagnation and your life starts to flow, too? A stream that starts to flow may come across obstacles, but as it pushes around and over

DAY 1
You Must Change If You Want Change

them, it continues to grow and become stronger. It grows from a small stream to a creek, then to a river, and from there it eventually flows into the ocean. Once a stream gets momentum there's no stopping it. As it grows, it allows more and more life to flourish within itself. Life around it flourishes, too.

Maybe you don't exactly feel like a raging torrent of life energy at the moment, but there's a stream inside of you with mighty potential. It's time to burst through the excuses that have held you back and let that stream flow by taking action. As it starts to flow you will see new life inside you.

No more damming up our stream with the excuses we have built up in the past. Today let's get real once and for all!

> *John 10:10: "The thief cometh not, but to steal, and to kill, and to destroy. I am come that they might have life and have it more abundantly."*

Today I want you to write out specifically what areas you need improvement in, whether it's self-esteem, weight, depression, or some other area. By day 91, if you follow through, you will see the change that up to now you've only wished for.

You Must Change If You Want Change

What Are You Waiting For?

Is there ever a good time to start anything? We like to procrastinate. At the same time, we are also the "NOW" generation, and we want instant results.

The problem with procrastination is our life is passing us by. Life is precious. Life is short. If we are fortunate enough to live into our early 80s, we will have had only about 30,000 days here to leave our legacy. Every day counts! We need to learn to live our life to the fullest.

When we procrastinate there's always an excuse behind it. For example, when the scale reads a certain number, I'd start to exercise—and only then. Or I'd say, "I'm so busy. Once things slow down, maybe I'll do something to make a difference." Here's one more:

"When the children are grown I'll take time out for myself."

If our statements start with "When this and when that," we are making excuses for not making things happen.

It's time to put our excuses aside and grab the bull by the horns. Take control of your life! Let's quit with "When this and when that" and start asking, "Why wait for this?" or "Why wait for that?" or how about "Why not start today?" No more excuses.

Let's look for reasons to go forward and quit looking for reasons to wait. You change your mind, you change your life! Today is a brand new day; past failures are in the past. Let's not make today another past failure. Choose to live differently today. Let's live our lives to the fullest.

What excuses have you made in the past?

_____

_____

_____

_____

_____

_____

DAY 2
What Are You Waiting For?

How can you choose to live differently today?

The Millionaire

Are you an optimist or a pessimist? Do you see the glass as half empty or half full? Do you know you are rich? That's right: you're already rich. It's all a matter of perspective.

Do you have your sight? Do you have your hearing? Can you walk? Can you talk? Can you move your limbs? Are there people in your life who love you? If you have any of these things, you're rich!

You don't think so? Well, let me ask you: would you sell your eyes for a million bucks? You wouldn't, would you? Because our eyes are precious. What about your hearing: would you give away your hearing for a million dollars? What about your legs or arms? Of course not; therefore, you are worth millions!

If you had something worth millions, how would you treat it? Would you never give it a second thought, or would you brag about it? Then why do you do the opposite when you look in the mirror?

Why do we say or think negative statements about ourselves? As of today let's view ourselves as we would that million-dollar item. Aren't we more precious than any material thing?

Today, reflect on what you have in your life, not on what you don't. Brag to yourself about how great you really are, just as if you were pointing out that million-dollar item to someone else.

You are that million-dollar item! Let your confidence soar. Enjoy this journey you have started, and be grateful for all you have. Tell yourself you will be grateful for every breath you are given, and resolve to live your life to the very best of your ability.

DAY 3
The Millionaire

Today's Exercise

What are you grateful for right now?

_____
_____
_____
_____
_____
_____
_____

List one thing you can change about the way you have looked at yourself in the past and how you plan to change your view from this point forward:

_____
_____
_____
_____
_____
_____
_____

4

Stop the Madness

If you keep doing what you've always done, you keep getting what you've always gotten. Here's the good news: if you want something different, you just have to make a different choice. It really is that simple.

As my favorite author and speaker, Zig Ziglar, says: "You are who you are and what you are by what has gone into your mind. You can change who you are and what you are by changing what goes into your mind." I believe this is true.

For every positive, we hear nineteen negatives. Think about it: we constantly tell our kids "stop it," "cut it out," "don't do that," and "no." Most of what we see on TV or the Internet is negative. We have to make a conscious effort to put positive things in. Positive in = positive out!

What if we started taking one hour a day to read or listen to something positive? I believe this would be a great way to bring about positive change in our lives.

I spend the time I have in my car every day listening to self-improvement material. I'm changing my life by taking small steps. Will you? Wouldn't these small changes make a difference in who you are and what you become? A journey of a thousand miles starts with one single step. Renew your mind, renew your life!

Interesting Data:

According to George Barna, by age twenty-one, it is estimated that people will have been exposed to more than 250,000 acts of violence through television, movies, and video games. And they will have viewed more than 2,000 hours of pornographic images.

Media exposure has raised people's willingness to experiment with substances that are harmful to mind and body, such as drugs, alcohol, and smoking. Hollywood also portrays pre-marital sex as normal when in fact it can be just as harmful as drugs or other self-destructive behavior.

DAY 4
Stop the Madness

Almost 80 percent of the TV commercials kids see each year are for fast food, candy, sugary cereals, and toys.

No wonder we are an overweight, devolving nation!

Let's stop the madness!

What positive input can you put into yourself to help renew your mind?

One Day at a Time

Are you struggling? Changing behavior isn't always easy. But changing a negative behavior to a positive one is always worth the effort.

God won't give you more than you can handle. Have faith that He who created you will be able to pull you through.

God uses people to change people. How can you help another through his or her struggles if you haven't gone through the same struggles? He wants you to overcome, so you can pass it on and help others.

Romans 8:31 asks, "If God be for us, who can be against us?" With God on your side how can you fail? If today you're struggling, reach out and ask for help. Matthew 7:7 says, "Ask, and it shall be given you; seek and ye shall find; knock, and it shall be opened unto you." If you asked for help as you struggled, then I believe it's time to rejoice: help is on the way.

If you have been helped, it's time to reach out and help others. That's why I'm writing this book. I've asked for help in my journey, and I've received it. Now I'm hoping to help others in their journey. As I've been given, I hope to give. If you and I can learn to live out this philosophy by helping others win, we win.

What struggles are you working on overcoming today?

_____
_____
_____
_____
_____
_____
_____
_____
_____
_____

DAY 5

One Day at a Time

1 Corinthians 10:13: "There hath no temptation taken you but such as is common to man: but God is faithful, who will not suffer you to be tempted above that ye are able; but will with the temptation also make a way to escape, that ye may be able to bear it."

Food Is Not Your Friend

Food *can* be your friend if you choose wisely. But I didn't always choose wisely.

What kind of friend would stab you in the back and do anything and everything to hurt you? Suppose this friend tried to harm your character, your career, and the image your friends and family have of you. Maybe your so-called friend brought you joy when you two were together. But what if your friend were up to no good behind your back? How long would he or she be your friend?

The food I once considered my friend brought me joy when it was before me on the plate. But once I actually ate it, the same food brought depression, heartburn, laziness, weakness in my body, and achy joints. Most importantly, it was bringing about a slow death. This food gave me only temporary happiness. Should I really have kept it on my Friends List?

Of course not. So why would I allow foods I know are harmful to be part of my diet? Worse than that, why did I deceive myself into thinking they are my friends?

I am a child of the most high God; therefore, there is no junk in me. Why, then, should I continue to put junk inside of me that does not belong?

Yesterday is history. I can't change the past, but I can learn from it. I can grow and make better choices. Here's the good news: the past does not have to define our future.

It's time to find some better friends. Let's try a healthy alternative today. Who knows? You might find a new best friend.

Today's challenge:

Find and make a new healthy recipe to replace an old friend.

Slow and Steady

Slow and steady wins the race. Maybe you didn't achieve what you wanted this first week. That's OK. Did you improve? There's a saying that goes, "How do you eat an elephant? One bite at a time." Well, your journey is taken one step at a time.

Remember the story of the tortoise and the hare? Your money should be on the rabbit, right? But the tortoise wins every time. Why is that? Because rabbits get off on rabbit trails. They start the course great, but when the going gets tough, they stray. Eventually they may get back on track, but often only to stray again.

Which have you been in the past—the tortoise or the hare? If you're not staying on the path, it's time to change, starting with your mind. Changing your mind will change your character. Then you can continue on the path you now have started down.

You can win the race! A slow pace is fine. If you're improving, you are well on your way to reaching your goals. Just keep moving forward and be persistent. James 1:8 tells us, "a double minded man is unstable in all his ways." Let's quit being double minded. No more going down the rabbit trail.

Fun fact:

Did you know tortoises have one of the longest life spans, up to 175 years old? Guess what they eat? Lots of greens.

Today's Challenge:

Add some greens to your diet starting today!

If You Slip, Don't Slide

Have you slipped up on your path toward your goals? Maybe you had a social gathering that you didn't prepare for properly and you messed up big time. Sometimes achieving your goals can feel like an uphill battle.

That's OK. If you slip going up that hill, get back up, dust yourself off, and keep going toward your goals. You may have slipped; just don't slide. When you slip, you can catch yourself and keep going up. But a slide takes you down the hill, away from your goal, back to the starting point. Don't give up—just keep going forward.

You will never get to your goals if you find yourself always back at the starting point. This is something I used to do. I would do great for a week or two. I would be well on my way to my destination, and then one little mess-up would send me into an eating frenzy. I would end up back at the starting point or sometimes even worse than where I originally started.

The problem is, when your slip keeps turning into a slide, eventually the hill seems to get bigger and bigger until it looks like a mountain. From this point let's accept that we might have a slip-up . . . but no more down slides.

What has been a slip food for you in the past?

_____

_____

_____

_____

_____

_____

_____

_____

_____

DAY 8
If You Slip, Don't Slide

What will you do to avoid a future slide?

Redeeming the Time

It's easy to grow stagnant in life, to become complacent. I think back to how many times my children asked me to play with them, and I would tell them not now, maybe later, simply because I was too lazy.

Sometimes I've been duped into thinking happiness is sitting in front of a TV set, stuffing my face with junk food (unconscious of just how much I was really eating), and living my life through the characters on the TV set.

Extreme Weight Loss and *Biggest Loser* were two of my favorite shows. Seeing people get their lives back was inspirational, but I was slowly frittering away my own life. Sitting on the sidelines watching others take action did nothing for me. Then one day I decided to get off the sidelines and take action myself.

You can read as many weight-loss books as you want, but until you apply what you read, all you have is knowledge. To me, knowledge is like gas in your car. Gas is necessary to get you where you want to go, but until you get in the driver's seat and put the key in the ignition, you aren't going anywhere.

No more watching others reclaim their lives while letting our own slip away. They're redeeming the time. They're redeeming their relationships, making time for their children, and creating lives to be proud of. Marriages get better, jobs become more fulfilling.

Now's *our* time! No more just watching others. Let's get off the couch and regain ourselves. Now is the time for others to watch *us*. We will redeem our relationships. Our marriages will get better. Our jobs will become more fulfilling.

This is your time to be proud of yourself. You have everything you need. You're in the driver's seat, and the gas tank's full. All you have to do is put the key in the ignition and start your journey. I hear the motor running; now step on the gas!

DAY 9
Redeeming the Time

Quote of the day:

You can ignore reality, but you can't ignore the consequences of ignoring reality.

—Ayn Rand

Be Like Mike

In 1992, Gatorade aired the "Be Like Mike" commercial. I'm not much of a basketball fan; however, almost everyone knows who Michael Jordan is. He's one of the greatest basketball players of all time. If you grew up playing the game, you probably dreamed of being as good as Mike. Let's see what Michael Jordan himself says about what it's like to be Mike.

> *I've missed more than 9,000 shots in my career. I've lost almost 300 games. Twenty-six times I've been trusted to take the game-winning shot and missed. I've failed over and over and over again in my life. And that is why I succeed.*
>
> —Michael Jordan

Did you catch that? He succeeded because he wasn't scared to fail. Through his failures he became great! Will you push through your failures and become great?

Did you know that the greatest basketball player of all time was cut from his high school basketball team because he wasn't good enough? What if he had let that failure define him? What if you let your past failures define you? Isn't it time to "Be Like Mike"?

Other Michael Jordan quotes:

Some people want it to happen, some wish it would happen, others make it happen.

The key to success is failure.

The minute you get away from fundamentals—whether it's proper technique, work ethic, or mental preparation—the bottom can fall out of your game, your school work, your job, whatever you're doing.

If you do the work, you get rewarded. There are no shortcuts in life.

DAY 10
Be Like Mike

*To learn to succeed,
you must first learn to fail.*

*Obstacles don't have to stop you. If you run
into a wall, don't turn around and give up.
Figure out how to climb it, go through it,
or work around it.*

*You must expect great things of yourself
before you can do them.*

Know and Do

To know how to do something and to actually do something are two different things. I believe you already know how to be successful in most things. But to follow through is a whole other matter.

For me, these ninety-one days are about my weight-loss journey. I have all the knowledge I need to succeed. I know about The Zone, South Beach, and Paleo diets. I've learned a little about raw foods and have been a member of Weight Watchers. Guess what? All of them worked. That's right, all of them worked for me—temporarily.

What didn't work was me. Let me explain: I dieted, but I didn't make a lifestyle change. "Die" is part of "diet." Eventually my commitment died off, and I went back to my old self.

In the end, I cared more about the pain from the diet or program I was on than about the pleasure of great health and looking and feeling good.

I learned in Weight Watchers that nothing tastes as good as healthy feels. Once you get your mind right, you can see that truth. Where your mind goes you will follow.

Here is an example of that. Jesus said in Matthew 5: 27–28: "Ye have heard that it was said by them of old time, Thou shalt not commit adultery; but I say unto you that whosoever looketh on a woman to lust after her hath committed adultery with her already in his heart." Looking will eventually become doing.

If I look at junk food long enough, I am going to eat it. Optimal health must be what brings me pleasure, not that pizza.

You already know what to do. That's why I'm not telling you how to eat or exercise. This book is a companion to what you already know about a healthy lifestyle. Most programs only give temporary results. We must learn to renew our mind if we want permanent change.

If I were to put a plate of food in front of you, I believe you probably already know if it would bring

DAY 11
Know and Do

you closer to your goals or drive you farther away. We know what's good for us and what's not. The problem lies with the mind. That's where this book comes in.

Renewing your mind is the key to renewing your life. What you dwell on is what you become. It's time to get your mind off fattening foods and on to a healthy you. That's the ultimate treat.

What do you know you should do but have chosen not to do?

What can you focus on to bring yourself closer to the goals you desire in your life?

What Kind of Person Are You?

All mankind is divided into three groups: those that are immovable, those that are movable, and those that move.

—Benjamin Franklin

I've been immovable or complacent for too long. Change will never happen without action. We must learn to move, toward things that are healthy and away from things that are destructive. Whether it's improving our health, our relationships, or our career, we must learn to move toward the things that will get us where we want to be.

If you want to accomplish anything, you must step over the ropes and into the ring. I'm tired of being immovable and watching others move on to better things. Aren't you? We've been spectators for far too long. It's time to get up and fight for what's important. Here's another quote I love.

> *There are three kinds of people in the world, the wills, the won'ts and the can'ts. The first accomplish everything; the second oppose everything; the third fail in everything.*
>
> —Eclectic Magazine

You may not always be one-hundred percent in one category, but which one do you tend to hang out in? You get to choose. Careful what you aim for because you will hit it every time. Here's one last quote for you to reflect on.

> *There are three types of people in this world: those who make things happen, those who watch things happen, and those who wonder what happened.*
>
> —Mary Kay Ash

DAY 12
What Kind of Person Are You?

Let's make things happen. As Garth Brooks sings in one of his songs, "Nothin' ventured, nothin' gained, sometimes you've got to go against the grain." So I'll ask you: Do you have the strength to go against the grain?

Today's challenge:

The above lyrics are from Garth Brooks's song "Against the Grain." I'm challenging you to download and listen to it today.

Fail to Plan, Plan to Fail

Once in a while, life is going to throw you under the bus. That's just life; it has nothing to do with you as a person.

Here's an example of an event that made me slip (but not slide). A close family member passed away. In all the rushing around to be with family and help out, I let my guard down. After we were finished making funeral arrangements, the family gathered together in the afternoon. I was famished. There was nothing really healthy to eat. Then someone ordered my favorite pizza.

Now, eating a slice or two wouldn't have been that big of a problem, but that piece or two became a problem as I found myself slipping into old habits and going back for "just one more." Things could have been worse, though. I dusted myself off from that slip, and I'm heading back uphill, chasing the goal that I have set for myself.

In the past I would have made a mountain out of this molehill and given up. Slips like these used to send me into a major slide. No more. As my mind changes I'll get stronger and stronger, and therefore my life will become better and better. I will become the person I want to be, and you can, too.

We all will have a slip from time to time, but the next time a slip comes your way, what are you going to do? Will it just be a slip, or will it become a slide into old habits that lead to an unfulfilled lifestyle?

Quote of the day:

If you want change you must get off the merry-go-round.

Don't Break

You may crack, your faith may be shaken, and at times it might even feel like the world is crashing in on you. Don't give up, don't stop. Persevere. As my wife says: through your misery comes your ministry; through your test comes your testimony.

To build muscle you have to persevere. A muscle is built up by being broken down. By being broken down it comes back stronger and stronger. You won't have a testimony without enduring the test. To have a ministry you have to overcome the misery.

As Dave Ramsey said, "Having a testimony is great; getting one is a pain in the butt." You've known pain but you've been stronger than it. If you weren't you wouldn't be reading this book. The strong survive. They overcome.

You are endowed with the seeds of greatness from your Father on high. Therefore, there's no junk in you! You may have cracks, but you're not broken. Break through and follow your dreams. Reach out with your testimony and help others.

But to be able to heal others, you must first heal yourself. Let's heal those wounds and then accomplish all you have set your mind to. Let the healing begin; you're worth it.

The Mirror

I'm grateful for my companion, my life partner, my wife, Kathy. She is such a source of support and encouragement in my life. Not all of you may be fortunate enough to have a spouse in your life right now, but for those of you who do, today's reading is for you.

In the Garden, God saw that it was not good for Adam to be alone. God made Adam a help mate from his rib. Notice not from his foot bone or from his skull. He is not to lord over her, nor is she to lord over him. They are to walk side by side.

Success will be only temporary until we get our marriages right. Our spouses are like mirrors: they reflect our own behavior and attitudes toward them. If there are things you don't like about your spouse, don't be mad at the reflections they're giving back. Take a long, hard look at yourself in the mirror. You very well may be receiving what you are giving.

Unless you are united with your other half, you will not be truly whole. Life is short and sometimes rough, so let's be grateful for our spouses. If you knew today was your last chance to say something to your spouse, what would you say? What would you do?

When you speak words of life to others, you reignite life in yourself. The mirror reflects what you show it. When you give, you receive. What can you give of yourself today?

If something has been lost along the way in your marriage, it can be rebuilt. If you want what you once had you have to do what you once did. To be successful in this journey, you must grow in all areas, and your marriage is one of the most important.

If there's heaviness in your marriage you will feel it in your body, your career, and in all areas of your life. So get started today on building a marriage that supports you instead of weighing you down.

DAY 15
The Mirror

How can you make your marriage lasting and a source of happiness and support?

What's Your Excuse?

As you may have picked up by now, this book is all about the mind. If you get your mind right, you can lose weight and accomplish amazing things.

Why do some people conquer seemingly insurmountable obstacles while others can't seem to conquer anything even if they have everything going for them?

One of those amazing people who seems to let nothing stand in his way is Nick Vujicic. Check him out at lifewithoutlimbs.org. After you do, I want you to ask yourself this: If this man can accomplish so much with the obstacles set before him, why not you?

Look at yourself. I'm guessing you have more going for you physically than Nick does. We have no more excuses. If you haven't started making major changes,

why not? The only difference between you and Nick is that you haven't set your mind to conquer your obstacles.

In reality, the challenge before each and every one of us is the battle going on inside our minds. Instead of saying "I can't" we need to learn to say "I can." At this point you may not know *how* you can, but say to yourself that you're going to find a way to accomplish what you've set your mind to. Saying "I can't" to ourselves is really just saying "I won't."

What if Nick said he can't? Where would he be? What if you keep saying you can't? Where will you be? I'm not saying "can't" this time. I can and I will—and you can, too!

Today's homework: Go to lifewithoutlimbs.org and check out Nick Vujicic.

If Nick can accomplish what he has, what can you accomplish in your life?

_____
_____
_____
_____
_____

DAY 16
What's Your Excuse?

What's the first or next step you are going to take to accomplish these goals?

Build a Puzzle

When you look at a completed puzzle you get a complete picture. What's the picture you have in your mind for your life? Close your eyes and really get that picture in your mind of a life that brings fulfillment. What would it look like?

You may have many pieces to your puzzle—family, career, personal achievement, and others. Whatever your puzzle looks like it will never be completed if you don't start adding a piece here and a piece there.

When you put together a puzzle you usually start by finding all the edge pieces and assemble the border first. Our lives get out of balance because we haven't got our borders in place. Can you imagine trying to put together a puzzle if the borders were added last? How hard would that be? It would be almost impossible, wouldn't it?

That's what I used to do. I would see a picture in the middle of the puzzle in my mind and try to make that picture a reality, but without doing the borders first. Hard to do! So now I make sure the borders are done before trying to complete the puzzle.

One border of my puzzle will be to put time aside every day for motivation and inspiration from books, tapes, and podcasts. Another side is to set goals, writing them down with deadlines. I will review them daily and set a plan in motion for how to accomplish them. The third side of my puzzle will be to get in some sort of physical activity every day to keep my energy, my focus, and my health in top form. And the final border is to strengthen my relationship with God, family, and friends. I believe with the borders in place that the picture I have imagined for myself can now be accomplished. Small steps make a big difference. Are you ready to take the next step?

DAY 17
Build a Puzzle

What does the picture you have in your mind for your perfect life look like?

What are the four borders you will put in place to complete the picture of your perfect life?

Is It Worth It?

Weight Watchers teaches that you need to count every "BLT": bite, lick, and taste. Here's an example of why. One M&M is approximately three calories, and in order to burn off those three calories, you would need to walk or run the length of one football field or one hundred yards. How many bite-sized morsels do we ingest in a day and don't even realize it?

For every one "fun-size" candy bar (Snickers, Milky Way, Butterfinger), each about eighty calories, you would need to walk around 0.8 miles or 1,600 steps to burn it off.

Exercise is important, but the weight will never come off permanently until we learn to eat differently. It takes twenty-six minutes of running to burn off one slice of pizza. So if we ate just what I've listed so far—one M&M, one snack-size Snickers, and one piece of pizza—it would take around thirty minutes of running and another thirty minutes of walking just to burn the calories.

A day like this in the past for me was a pretty good day with not a ton of bad choices. However most days I would hit fast food at least once and sometimes as many as 3 to 4 times. My career requires me to be on the road a lot. So fast food was convenient. But was it worth it?

Topping out at 260 pounds, well on my way to 300, it was time for a change. A Big Mac extra value meal would take around two hours and fifteen minutes of running or five and a half hours walking to burn off. So in order to burn off that whole meal you would have to do about a half marathon! That's 13.1 miles! That's just one meal. Not even super-sized.

And to think I would go through the drive-thru five to fifteen times a week. That's a lot of marathons each week.

I used to make the excuse that I didn't have time to pack a lunch. But if I don't have five minutes to pack a lunch, I sure don't have five hours to work it off.

If I don't plan, I'd better plan to fail. But failure is no longer an option for us. We have three choices: 1) spend five to ten minutes to make out a game plan

DAY 18
Is It Worth It?

for that day for our meals. 2) Run a half to a whole marathon every day. 3) Stay fat.

I'm choosing #1. How about you?

What did your daily food intake look like in the past?

_____

_____

_____

_____

_____

_____

_____

What kind of changes can you implement to make sure you're getting the proper nutrition your body needs?

_____

_____

_____

_____

_____

_____

_____

Let It Erupt

There's a volcano inside of you waiting to erupt. You are so much more powerful than you think you are. Let it erupt—be strong and accomplish the goals you set out for yourself.

No one's holding you back but you. But if anybody does try to hold you back—we all know misery loves company—don't let them.

You're in control. You're in the driver's seat. Who wants to stay miserable?

Get inspired and reach for the sky. Try something new. You have only one life to live, and this isn't a dress rehearsal. Who knows? You may find something you enjoy.

I'm finding out I actually like to jog. Who knew? I started small and by day 19 did eight miles between walking and jogging on the treadmill. In the past if you would have told me I could do this I would have said no way.

Where there's a will there's a way. Make a way for what you want in your life. Let that volcano erupt and break through those past limitations you have set on yourself. You can do anything you want if you set your mind and your heart to it.

There's a saying: "If you think you can, you're right!" If you think you can't, you're also right. Which type of person (the can or the can't) will you be from this point on?

What are some limitations you have put on yourself in the past?

_____

_____

_____

_____

_____

_____

DAY 19
Let It Erupt

What can you do to break through those limitations?

The Lifesaver

Slogans are a lifesaver in times of need. In this book I've included a lot of slogans I've picked up through the years. My wife and her dad have tons of great slogans, some of which appear in this book.

Slogans have always been motivating for me. They inspire. They can get you through the tough times and the sad times. They can help bring happiness and peace of mind. Even the Bible has a few verses you could consider slogans. Here are a few.

Psalms 46:10: "Be still and know that I am God."

Philippians 4:13: "I can do all things through Christ which strengtheneth me."

Proverbs 22:6: "Train up a child in the way he should go: and when he is old, he will not depart from it."

Deuteronomy 31:6: "Be strong and of good courage, fear not, nor be afraid of them: for the Lord thy God, he it is that doth go with thee: he will not fail thee, nor forsake thee."

John 10:10: "The thief cometh not, but for to steal, and to kill, and to destroy: I am come that they might have life, and that they might have it more abundantly."

These are verses that can bring peace and comfort. They are words of blessing and bring about life. There are hundreds if not thousands of these throughout the Bible you can draw upon in time of need.

DAY 20
The Lifesaver

The next slogans are not found in the bible but are still good to draw upon for inspiration.

> *"It's not who you think you are that's holding you back; it's who you think you're not."*

> *"Tough times don't last, tough people do."*

> *"If it doesn't challenge you, it doesn't change you."*

> *"Suffer the pain of discipline or suffer the pain of regret."*

> *"If you really want to do something, you'll find a way. If you don't, you'll find an excuse."*

So there you have it, some great words of inspiration to meditate on and inspire yourself today. It doesn't matter what you've done in the past; live in the present and change your future. You're the one who can make all the difference in the world. Now go do it.

Today's Challenge:

Find a slogan you can meditate on that will help you be inspired today!

Forming New Habits

Congratulations! You've made it twenty-one days. It's said that it takes twenty-one days to form a new habit. Have you formed any new habits in the last twenty-one days?

Old habits are hard to break, but if you keep moving forward, your new habits will in time become new-old habits you won't want to break because they will bring out the best of you.

The Army has a slogan that goes, "Be all you can be. You can do it in the Army." Nothing wrong with the Army, but you don't need the Army to be all you can be.

What you need to be all you can be is to develop new habits to replace unproductive old habits. Tom

Ziglar puts it this way: "The fastest way to success is to replace bad habits with good habits."

We all want success but, as Henry Ford said, "If you always do what you've always done, you'll always get what you've always gotten." I don't believe you want what you've always gotten, otherwise you would not have picked up this book. I'm changing my habits. Will you?

What are some new habits you have developed in the last twenty-one days?

_____
_____
_____
_____
_____
_____
_____
_____
_____
_____
_____
_____
_____

DAY 21

Forming New Habits

What new habits could you start to develop in the next twenty-one days that would help move you closer to your goals?

Step Up to the Plate

You have to love yourself if you want lasting change. As The Beatles put it, "All you need is love."

I bet you have someone in your life you love so much that if it came down to it, you'd lay down your life for that person. Jesus said, "Greater love hath no man than this, that a man lay down his life for his friends." You might think you would lay down your life for a friend or a loved one. But will you lay down your bad habits for the sake of a better life?

We all have just one life to live, so why not step outside the box? Take a chance to accomplish your dreams. Nothing great happens without somebody stepping up to the plate. Sure, you could strike out. It's possible. But you're never going to be a hero sitting on the sidelines. If you want to hit a home run, you have to step up to the plate. Heroes don't become heroes without a few strikeouts. Heroes become heroes because they're willing to strike out. They get into the game. We've been on the sidelines far too long. Isn't it time to step up to the plate?

Love yourself enough to step out of your comfort zone. Chances are you will learn to love your life by your willingness to go for it. You have everything to gain and very little to lose. Go gain what life has for you.

Life's an adventure; be adventurous and make your dreams your new reality. A dream is just a future reality. If you don't chase after it, your dream remains only a dream.

Start turning your dreams into reality today. If you have the right vision, I believe the Lord will give you the provision you need. So, batter up!

DAY 22
Step Up to the Plate

What's something you could do right now that's outside your comfort zone?

How will that empower your life?

Hope-Wish-Want

"Hope to," "wish to," or "want to" are not true commitments. With such statements you're on the road to failure every time.

We need to watch our thoughts; they become our words. We need to watch our words; they become our actions. And our actions will become our character, good or bad.

Constantly saying "I couldn't do that" or "I wish I could do that" turns our desires into wishes that never come true.

Think of people you admire. The reason you admire them is probably because they have learned to control their thoughts and be positive. Their words empower them and others. They say things like, "I'm going to" or "I can" or "I will accomplish this."

Since their thoughts have become their words, their words have become their actions, their actions have become their habits, which become their character.

It all started with the thought. Greatness starts with the thought of greatness. If you think you can, you can. If you want to be a role model, if you want to be empowered, start with your thoughts.

What new thought patterns can you adopt into your life today?

_____
_____
_____
_____
_____
_____
_____
_____
_____
_____
_____
_____

DAY 23
Hope-Wish-Want

How will that have an effect on your character?

Don't Fear

What would you do if you weren't afraid?

Fear holds us back from our dreams. Fear and faith are opposing forces. Unless you can muster up more faith than fear, fear will win. It will hold you back every time.

We often know what we should do, but then fear takes hold and we become stuck. We become complacent.

If you don't overcome your fears, you will stay ordinary instead of becoming extraordinary.

You know, most things I've worried about in my life never came to pass. **FEAR** is simply **False-Evidence-Appearing-Real.** Fear used to hold me back from my dreams. No more.

How about you? Will you embrace fear or faith?

What are some past fears that have held you back?

Write about a situation when faith helped you overcome a fear that was holding you back.

What It Takes

I would guess that you probably already know that an average meal should range from about 300 to 500 calories (depending on a few different factors like your age, sex, weight) when you eat three meals per day. We should also have around two snacks per day at about 100 to 200 calories each. As you may already know, it's good to eat about every three hours.

I'm not giving diet advice here or telling you what to eat or what to do to lose weight. What I want all of us to do is to start to view food differently.

You can eat a lot of food for 300 to 500 calories, if you choose the right food. But if you choose the wrong food, just a few bites will get you to 300 to 500 calories with little or no nutrition.

Here's a hard fact: it takes about a mile of running to burn off 100 calories. So a meal that contains 900 calories has an excess of 400 calories. So in order for us to burn that off we would have to run four miles! Does knowing this make you want to be a little more careful with your food choices?

Wouldn't it be nice if instead of restaurant menus listing 1,200 calories next to a meal they listed "seven miles." Meaning, in order to burn off the excess of 700 calories you would have to run seven miles. I bet we'd be a lot more selective.

So next time you look at a menu board and see 900 calories for a meal, you have three choices. Choice 1: pick something different. Choice 2: eat half the meal and box the other half for a later meal. Or Choice 3: eat the meal and go jog four miles to burn off the excess calories. Next time you're making a meal choice, remember: You do have a choice! Your choices will ultimately lead to your destiny. What is your destiny?

DAY 25
What It Takes

Here's what it takes!

FOOD	CALORIES	FAT
McDonald's Big Mac	**563**	**33**
McDonald's medium-size French fry	**384**	**20**
McDonald's medium-size vanilla shake	**733**	**21**
Total for one meal:	**1,680 cal.**	**74**

Distance to run to burn off excess calories: 11 to 12 miles

FOOD	CALORIES	FAT
Burger King Whopper with cheese	**790**	**48**
Burger King medium-size French fry	**387**	**20**
Burger King medium-size vanilla shake	**733**	**21**
Total for one meal:	**1,844 cal.**	**103**

Distance to run to burn off excess calories: 13 to 14 miles

Hardest or Easiest

Is there anything you can do right now to make your life worse?

If you answered yes to that question, there must also be something that you can do right now to make your life better. You can choose to overcome, or you can be overcome.

During my career in sales, I've learned that sales can be the hardest easiest work there is. Losing weight is much the same. It is easy to lose weight, but mentally it can be really hard.

Tony Robbins, in his personal power program, talks about two motivating forces in our life: pain and pleasure. He says that most people will do more to avoid pain than they will to gain pleasure.

Tony gives a few examples of how pain and pleasure work in our life. Here's one. Have you ever seen an attractive person you would like to ask out, but the pain of possible rejection keeps you from approaching that person? Even though having this person in your life might bring massive pleasure, we choose to avoid the pain of rejection instead.

We think the situation will probably bring us more pain than pleasure. The pain stops us dead in our tracks. But what if we could change the way we viewed things?

For example, how painful would it be if this person were never in our life? If we saw that more pain will result from not asking this person out, we may very well be moved to go for it.

The pleasure-pain principle is also part of the reason why we don't lose the weight. We start viewing the diet or the healthy food as involving too much pain and the unhealthy stuff as bringing more pleasure.

What if we became conscious of just how much pain unhealthy foods really cause us? There's the pain of never being healthy, the pain of being overweight if we keep eating the same way we always have. The pain of being depressed and sick. The pain of letting our loved ones down.

Imagine, too, if we started to see the pleasure we experience on our journey to health. There's the pleasure

DAY 26
Hardest or Easiest

of lots of energy and the pleasure of having massive joy in our life.

If we could learn to change our associations with food, losing weight wouldn't be the hardest thing to do anymore; it might be the easiest.

List something in the past you knew you should do but which the pain of possible failure or rejection involved kept you from moving forward:

Hardest or Easiest

How painful will it be if you don't ever move forward in that area but let fear continue to keep you down?

Day 27

Be Honest

How many times in our lives have we told ourselves or others that we can't do something? You know, oftentimes what we say we can't do is really something we could if we tried. When we say we can't, we are saying we have no control, that it's out of our hands.

When you think you can't, you are absolutely 100 percent correct. You will never overcome anything that you believe you can't overcome. But what if you started telling yourself the truth? What if you replaced "I can't" with "I won't?" At least then you'd be telling yourself the truth.

Once you realize you have the power to choose "I won't" or "I will," there's a chance you will move from "I won't" to "I will." However, as long as you keep telling yourself you can't, you are saying to yourself you don't have the power to choose, that it's out of your hands, and that whatever happens, happens.

When you say you can't, you become stuck. When you feel stuck, you get complacent. When you get complacent, you stop dreaming. When you stop dreaming, you get depressed. And when you get depressed, you get sick—all from saying just one little word: *can't*.

Learn to change your language. When you change your language, your life changes. From now on, instead of saying "I can't," let's at least be honest with ourselves and say "I can" or "I won't."

You are in control, and there's no one else and no other circumstance you can point to as the reason for not accomplishing what you know you should but have chosen not to.

No more lying to yourself. It's time to be honest: you either will or you won't. From this point on, no more *can't* allowed.

Holiday Time

Plan and prepare healthy choices. Have a game plan and stick to it.

That said, I know it can be difficult during a holiday or festive celebration. There are birthdays, anniversaries, Thanksgiving, summer BBQs, and all the national holidays.

We may have an average of ten or fifteen meals per year we could potentially stumble over. Was it these meals that made us fat, or was it our overall lifestyle? If we eat three meals per day on average, that's 1,095 meals per year. If we slip up on only fifteen meals a year or less, that's only 1 percent of our meals in a whole year. Did 1 percent really make us fat?

I used to say that the holiday meals killed me. But the cold, hard fact is that a few holiday meals didn't kill me. What killed me was the other 99 percent. As we discussed on day 8, a slip won't hurt, but a slide will.

We like to say things like, "I'll be glad once the new year is here and we are finally through the holidays so I can get back on track. I've put on so much weight this holiday season." Here's what's funny: I never once said, "I'll be glad when Tuesday's over so I can get back on track." I also never said, "Those Wednesdays and Thursdays kill me every time." That would be about as crazy as blaming a holiday like Thanksgiving for our weight.

We have to remember that it's not a single day or season that got us this way. It's our lifestyle. So, again, plan and prepare healthy choices for these gatherings. Go in with a game plan and stick to it. If we happen to slip a little, that's OK. Let's just keep it at a slip and not a slide. With a slip, we can catch ourselves and keep moving forward, but a slide hurts and hurts bad!

DAY 28
Holiday Time

When was the last time a slip in your eating became a slide into days, weeks, even months of continuing in that same destructive pattern?

How hard was it to rebound from that slide?

DAY 28
Holiday Time

What will you do differently to make sure your next slip doesn't turn into a slide?

The Secret

What's the secret to successful weight loss? A 2008 study in the *American Journal of Preventive Medicine* showed that keeping a food diary can double your chances of success. Researchers from Kaiser Permanente's Center for Health Research kept tabs on 1,685 overweight and obese adults and, after twenty weeks, the average weight loss was thirteen pounds per person. However, researchers discovered something else: the more participants recorded what they ate, the more weight they lost in the end. Participants who did not keep a food diary lost about nine pounds over the course of the study, while those who recorded their food intake six or more days per week lost eighteen pounds, twice as much as those who didn't keep track.

That goes along with the Weight Watchers' philosophy that you need to record every BLT (bite, lick, taste).

When you write down your activities, you can review them. It's kind of the same with goals. A goal isn't a goal unless it's written down. Unless you have it down on paper, it's just a dream. The dream of weight loss will become a reality by having clearly defined goals written down. Then you can track your progress on a daily basis.

We can get where we want to go twice as fast by writing it down. Wouldn't it be worth five minutes of effort a day to reach your goals faster? This is such a simple secret; yet most won't do it because it takes a little extra effort. But the rewards are worth the effort, aren't they? You decide.

What's keeping you from recording your progress toward your goals?

_____
_____
_____
_____
_____

DAY 29
The Secret

What would be the benefits of keeping such a record?

Day 30

What's Eating You?

I imagine there are areas in your life that leave you feeling unfulfilled. I know there were in my life. Otherwise I wouldn't have been about seventy-five pounds over my ideal weight.

I made food my escape. Some people turn to drugs and alcohol. I chose food. I would overeat when I was happy, sad, angry, or depressed.

Sometimes we had a different vision for our lives when we were young. We thought things would be different, and then we got caught up with the daily struggles in our life. We got busy and let a little part of ourselves go.

There have been times when I've emotionally neglected my wife and children because I got caught up in this or that. Tough times would always follow, and I'd turn to food.

There have also been times in my career when I felt unappreciated or unfulfilled. Again I would turn to food. I'd be on my way home from work, maybe fifteen miles from my house, run through a drive-thru, and start on my way home. Only minutes from home, I'd eat my meal, pass by my house, and drive another three miles to the next town—to find another drive-thru! That's insanity. I just ate 20 minutes ago. So now I eat my second meal in five minutes or less and then walk in the door to my house only to go to the refrigerator to see what there is to eat. This was not normal eating, for nutrition. This was emotion-driven.

Sometimes we feel like we've been in quicksand too long and we're going down. We give up. But don't give up. Get up. Fight for what's important.

You can have the marriage you want, the family, the career. We need to learn to take the time to make these things happen and make them great.

At 260 pounds I actually could see myself in my mind becoming 300-plus pounds before I could see myself at 200 pounds. I almost admitted defeat. So what changed? I'm learning to put positive things in my mind, which is helping to change my self-image. A better self-image, in turn, is helping to change my attitude. And since my attitude is improving, everything around me is getting better day by day.

I'm learning to confront the things that once bothered me and not just retreat into food. My life's becoming better. Yours can, too! We only live once. Let's live more fully, let's have more passion, let's work on those areas that need to be worked on. And let's start today!

What's something you have buried inside yourself, something you avoid a confrontation with by turning to food?

What's something you can do to start to release that hurt today and bring about healing?

Be Not Defined by a Number

Congratulations! You have made it a full thirty days. You may not be where you want to be by this point, but you should be well on your way.

Don't let a number on the scale define you. It's just a number. By this point you should be feeling better mentally, spiritually, and physically. You may also have more energy than you did thirty days ago.

For myself, I've noticed that after these thirty days I don't get heartburn anymore. For me this is fantastic; I used to down Mylanta and eat Tums and Rolaids like candy. I even had a doctor tell me after doing an upper scope procedure that I maybe ought to undergo surgery that would keep the acid from going up into

my esophagus. But all I had to do was make better food choices. I'm glad now I chose not to have surgery.

I also went with a friend once to a seminar about a medical procedure for losing weight. While there, you listened to testimonials, and then they would see if you were a candidate for the procedure. I don't remember the name of the procedure, but it was similar to having your stomach stapled.

I didn't think I would be heavy enough to qualify. After all, I was there for someone else. But they told me I was a prime candidate.

Thank God I didn't get that surgery, either. There is a better path than going under the knife. We have become such an "instant" society. We want it now and don't want to put in the work. But where is the reward in that?

We're strong enough to accomplish amazing feats. I hope you are seeing improvements in your health, too. Hopefully you're feeling better in all areas of your life. It's more than just how we look. It's how we feel and how we can bring joy to ourselves and to those around us.

I want to live my life to the fullest, so for me this time it's not about a number on the scale. It's about making a difference in myself, my career, and for those around me. I'm not there yet, but I'm on my way.

Let's quit defining ourselves by a number because we can all be #1.

Victim or Victorious

Some of us have been literally to hell and back. Some have had parents who divorced. Some had parents who withheld affection. They may have never told us they're proud of us or that they love us. Some of us had parents who were alcoholics or were really never around. And some of us have experienced the unimaginable—rape or other serious trauma.

These things may have caused us to turn to food. It's easy to let trauma define us and to become victims. Past wounds aren't our fault, but for some reason we tend to hold on to the baggage. Instead of letting it go, we let it eat at us. And then we in turn start to eat our way to self-destruction. Doesn't it get tiring?

We are products of our upbringing. The Bible tells us that the sins of the father can be passed down to the third and fourth generation. If our parents divorced, then statistically we have a greater chance ourselves of going through a divorce. If our parents had a problem with alcoholism or drugs, it very well may be a problem for us that might get passed down to our children, too.

It doesn't have to be that way, though. Through my teenage years into my mid-twenties, alcohol became an escape for me. It was a learned trait passed down. I soon realized as I had children that this wasn't how I wanted to raise my family, so I gave it up.

Unconsciously, however, I turned to food. It became my escape. It seemed to bring comfort. But the end results—depression, sickness, and obesity—weren't very comforting.

I victimized myself over things I really had no control over. I may not be able to change my upbringing, but I can choose to live differently. I had given up a negative to pick up another negative. I gave up drinking to replace it with overeating.

Today, I'm learning to live differently. When I give up a negative, I will replace it with something positive.

At one point the sins were being passed down from the past generation to my generation and could have continued to the next generation. Here's a secret

DAY 32
Victim or Victorious

to breaking the generational curse. Get a new father. Not an earthly father but a heavenly Father. God loves you and wants only the best for you. He will give you the power to overcome. You can turn over to God all that baggage you've been carrying. We no longer have to be victims. God will give you the victory. You can and will be victorious.

What are some burdens you have inherited from a previous generation?

What positive action can replace a negative one in your life?

Are We Not Better?

Some birds can fly more than one thousand miles back to the place they started from, even to the same nest. How is it they can hit their mark each time—even with such a little bitty brain?

Even with the most advanced computer system in nature between our ears, we often miss our mark. How do birds accomplish their remarkable feat? I'd like to say because they are guided by a greater power. If they can hit the mark, how much more can we?

The Lord tells us in Matthew 6:26, "Behold the fowl of the air: for they sow not, neither do they reap, nor gather into barns; yet your Heavenly Father feedeth them. Are you not much better than they?" The Lord takes care of them, and He goes on to say, "Are we not better?" If God takes care of the birds, He will take care of us.

I don't believe the Lord wants us unfit, unhealthy, and depressed. We can reach our goals as long as they are not contrary to God's will. If He can direct a bird to its nest from more than a thousand miles away—if that bird can hit its target—can't God enable us to hit our targets?

When we get spiritually fit, when we get mentally fit, we can get physically fit. 1 Corinthians 3:16 tells us, "Know ye not that ye are the temple of God, and that the Spirit of God dwelleth in you?" God's house is a house of order, not a house of chaos. When you align the physical, mental, and spiritual, you can accomplish amazing things.

Sometimes I think we forget we are designed to overcome, to attain greatness, and be successful. We are designed to have strong marriages and families and to be blessed as long as we walk in the ways of the Lord. Deuteronomy 28:13: "And the Lord shall make thee the head, and not the tail; and thou shall be above only, and thou shall not be beneath: if that thou hearken unto the commandments of the Lord thy God, which I command thee this day, to observe and to do them."

In summary, the Lord says: we are better than the birds; we are the head and not the tail. We are to be above

DAY 33
Are We Not Better?

and not beneath. We are the Temple of God, and He wants to dwell with us. Are we not better than the way we have treated ourselves? Should we talk negatively about ourselves, knowing we are the Temple of God? Let's not profane the Temple of God with negative self-talk. If the Lord is on your side, and you're doing your part to get mentally and physically fit, then I believe your target is in sight, and getting clearer and clearer every day.

What's something you can work on to get more spiritually fit?

What's something you can work on to get more mentally fit?

What's something you can work on to get more physically fit?

Get Long-Term Vision

I was recently listening to the Zig Ziglar podcast when I heard Tom Ziglar quote his dad as saying, "People trade what they want most for what they want now." How true is that?

For years, I wanted to take the weight off, but I traded what I wanted most for the love of food, indulging while moving farther away from my true desires. I wanted to look and feel good, but the food won out most times. I often used food to self-medicate, and over time the results weren't pretty.

There's a story in the Bible about how Esau sold his birthright for a bowl of pottage. God hated Esau because he despised his birthright. Have we at times despised our birthright?

DAY 34
Get Long-Term Vision

We are the children of God and designed for great things, so why have I sold a healthy lifestyle in the past for a taste of this and a taste of that? How come our vision is so short term? We need to get long-term vision and learn to trade what we want now for what we want most.

Every battle you win will bring you closer to victory in the war. We are built to be over-comers. Let's get some long-term vision and win the battles over what we want now so we can win the war for what we really want!

The next time what you want right now presents itself to you and is contrary to what you want most, what will you do to win the battle?

_____
_____
_____
_____
_____
_____
_____
_____
_____
_____
_____

Negative or Positive?

When you come out from one of life's storms, you won't be the same person you were when you entered it. That's the meaning of these storms.

In the past, my negativity led me into the storms of life. An example is with my work. I do in-home sales, and when I wasn't in the right frame of mind, I sometimes decided not to make an important call or prospect the way I should. Instead, I'd go home early. These decisions affected my income, which would bring on a bout of depression. Being depressed would then turn me to what I would have considered in the past as comfort food. One negative decision seemed to lead to another until I was in the whirlwind of life.

Well, if this is true, then the opposite must also be true. One positive decision leads to another. Dwelling on positives can affect our income, our families, and even our waistlines in a good way. When you're positive and learn to stay positive even when it seems everything is going wrong, you will impact the world for the better.

Your positivity will rub off on others, who will then, in turn, pass that positivity on to still others, and on and on in a chain reaction of positivity. You can affect hundreds if not thousands just by being positive.

Your daily actions will shape you for years and decades and even the generations after you. It's time to get rid of negativity and make positive behaviors a part of our daily routine.

Think of someone you really admire. I bet he or she is positive at least most of the time.

There used to be a character on *Saturday Night Live* years ago called Debbie Downer. She could and would bring negativity into any situation. When you think of the legacy you want to leave, what does it look like? Do you want to leave a legacy like Debbie Downer, where all you're known for is negativity? Or would you like to be known as someone who could find the good in all situations, someone people admire and aspire to be like?

DAY 35
Negative or Positive?

Your thoughts will determine your legacy. What will yours be: a negative one or a positive one?

What's a negative thought or behavior that you will eliminate from your life and replace with a positive thought or behavior?

Day 36

Get Your Guard Up

In this journey, I would guess you have made a few mistakes. Mistakes don't have to define us. They are just something that happen; they don't have to turn into a lifestyle.

In the past, eating something bad or unhealthy that wasn't on my diet plan would move me farther from my goals. I would continue in that destructive behavior for days, weeks, and sometimes even months before I would get back on track. *That's Crazy Thinking!*

That's like a boxer getting into the ring, letting his guard down so that he gets punched in the face, and then saying to himself, "Ouch, that hurt! Maybe I should put my guard back up, but before I do, I think I'll take several more blows to the head, and then maybe next round, if I survive, I'll put my guard up again." That would be crazy. That's not how the boxer would think, however. He would shake off the first punch and look to rebound right away by putting his guard right back up.

Let's learn to rebound right away from our mistakes in this ring of life. Instead of getting knocked out, let's get our guard back up. No more letting mistakes define us as a person. We are so much more than our mistakes!

Thought of the day:

Philippians 4:13: I can do all things through Christ which strengtheneth me.

Fight for Your Right

When I was a teenager, the Beastie Boys came out with the song, "(You Gotta) Fight for Your Right (to Party!)." I say you have to fight for your right to be healthy!

Have you joined the fight? With all the decisions we have to make daily about how to eat, being healthy will not happen on its own. We have to plan to be healthy; we have to overcome our obstacles. We have to learn to move our bodies and prepare our meals.

Fifty years ago, most jobs would require manual labor. Today, the majority of jobs involve sitting at a desk and staring at a computer screen.

While our activity level has gone down, our food intake has gone up. There are more and more unhealthy food choices now. You have fast food on almost every corner. Grocery stores are filled with mostly prepackaged foods that contain lots of chemicals. The produce section is shrinking in almost every store you go to. You really do have to fight for your right to be healthy nowadays.

Here's the good news, though: when you have to fight to accomplish something, it becomes that much more meaningful. Let's fight for health and appreciate what the Lord has given us. He has given most of us a healthy body that can accomplish amazing things. With our bodies we can stand up and fight; we can overcome and break down barriers and obstacles that seem immovable.

It all starts with one person—you! You can overcome and be a blessing to others, you can help others overcome and be able to break through the barriers that have held them back. You are strong; if you were not, then you would've put this book down way before now.

I'm becoming strong, too. Otherwise, this book wouldn't have made it into your hands. This is a battle we both can win. Let's put our strength together and go out and win our battles.

What's something small you can implement in your daily life that would up your activity level?

Concentrate on the Fundamentals

Anyone who is great in their field practices the fundamentals. They didn't just get great; they had to work at it every day. The same is true with our weight-loss journey.

We don't get physically fit without practicing the fundamentals. We instinctively know what the fundamentals are. We just like to ignore them.

Do you not already know you should move more? Of course, you do! We have to practice the fundamentals and schedule in the time to do what's healthy for us daily. Have you scheduled in exercise time daily yet? If not, why not?

We need to find the fun in the *fun*damentals. What do you enjoy? Can you incorporate something you enjoy into an exercise routine? Fun runs are becoming a new craze. There's everything from warrior runs to glow-and-bubble runs to even zombie runs. Why not try one? You never know—you might enjoy it!

Another fundamental would obviously be food preparation. Why not take a cooking class? It might become a new passion. You could learn to make amazing creations, anything from natural raw deserts that are very tasty and nutritious, to even learning about how to grow wheat grass, how to juice it—and why you would ever even want to.

We need to learn to make the fundamentals not an "I have to" but an "I want to." Maybe joining a sports team, or taking a cycling or karate class would also be fun. You never know what you have been missing until you give it a try.

There are many ways to tackle the weight, but it all boils down to the basics. Move more, make better food choices, and burn more calories than you take in. Pretty simple, huh? Now let's put the fun back into the fundamentals, and by day 91 you could be looking at a whole new you!

DAY 38

Concentrate on the Fundamentals

What's something you can do to put the fun back into the fundamentals?

Dig Deep

Do you want it bad enough?

When the going gets tough, what do you do? Do you do that extra rep, or do you throw in the towel and call it quits? Do you look for the easy way out and quit showing up for workouts?

There are going to be struggles throughout your entire life, and they are your opportunity to grow. You can take the easy way out, but if you do, you will never become the person you want to be. We need to learn to dig down deep. That needs to become our fuel, our motivation.

"When the going gets tough, the tough get going"—an overused saying, but so true. This is the time. This is the moment that shapes you and defines you. You put forth the effort, you get the results. All it takes is action!

Ask yourself a year from now what you are going to wish you had done today. Quit letting fear stand in the way of your dreams. Follow through on the decisions you have made. Hard work brings big results. Little work gets little results. Do you want small or big results? What are you willing to do to achieve your dreams?

It's easy to quit, but it's way more rewarding to look back on your life and know you did everything you could to accomplish your goals. What's hard is to let your life pass you by and live with the regret. Will you give it your all, or will you fall into the same old trap of self-defeat and one day look back wishing you'd done it all differently?

What's a fear that's been holding you back?

What's something you can do today to start to conquer that fear?

Take Action

The movers and shakers of this world take action. We can't become successful without taking action ourselves.

Ever noticed that it takes more energy to start an action then it does to keep it going? Beginnings are always the hardest. Getting started might hurt, but don't give up. Getting a ship, a train, or even a rocket up and moving takes a lot of force in the beginning, but once it gets going, it's easier to keep it going. A body in motion tends to stay in motion.

We have to give of ourselves in order to receive. If you give 100 percent in your workouts and your nutrition, you will have, 100 percent, the body you have always wanted.

You've heard the saying, "No guts, no glory." Most people don't have the guts to accomplish their goals. They have become complacent. But why accept a so-so life when we can have an extraordinary one?

Do you have the guts to change? Will you dig deeper than ever before? If you put forth the effort, you will be rewarded in the end. Today, put forth more effort than you have in the past and build on it every day. If you started improving 1 percent a day for the next 100 days, imagine where you would be. Visualize the new you, and embrace that vision.

If you will live by stretching yourself every day, you will become the best you that you can be. You will be blessed and empowered to enrich others. Plus, you will be able to look back and live with no regrets. Take action today!

What's an area in your life you have been complacent in?

_____
_____
_____
_____

DAY 40
Take Action

What can you do right now to change that?

Friend or Foe

Show me who you hang out with, and I'll show you who you are.

You may have heard this saying in the past. There happens to be a lot of truth to it. Whoever we hang out with is who we will become like. I heard someone say once that we often pay more attention to what we eat than who we eat with.

Sometimes people will try to hold you back, especially if they see that you are changing your life. They may feel like you're leaving them behind, so they will say negative, hurtful statements to try to sabotage your success. Don't let that bother you. Hurting people hurt people. If they see that you're accomplishing more than they are, they may see themselves as lesser. Not knowing how to handle their emotions, they lash out at you and try to drag you down to their level. Misery loves company.

I once heard Zig Ziglar say, "Don't be distracted by criticism. Remember—the only taste of success some people have is when they take a bite out of you." Don't let others pull you down because they don't like that you're changing. Everybody has the same opportunity as you do. The difference is you have decided to be more, have more, and give more. You have decided to be the right kind of person and change what you dwell on.

We will no longer be Nick Negative. We'll find the positives hidden even in the bad situations. There are positives even if it doesn't feel like it—I promise!

Positive people hanging out with negative people is like oil trying to mix with water. If you find that the people you're hanging out with aren't uplifting you, then it may be time to find new friends.

Successful people hang out with successful people. Want a good marriage? Hang out with people who have a good marriage. You want to be fit? Then hang out with people who work on their fitness. Birds of a feather flock together. Who do you want to flock with, the buzzards or the eagles?

Friend or Foe

Who builds you up in your life?

Who tears you down in your life?

What can you do to get more eagles to flock with and fewer buzzards?

Smile Today

Between 1937 and 2012, an estimated 1,600 bodies were recovered of people who had jumped from the Golden Gate Bridge to commit suicide. On average, somebody jumps from the bridge every two weeks.

In a sermon I heard recently, a man planned his suicide. He left a note at his house that said he was going to walk to the Golden Gate Bridge and jump. However if just one person would give him a smile on his way to the bridge, he would not jump. In his letter he expressed that just one smile would give him enough hope in humanity to make him change his course. Unfortunately the man jumped.

I've heard it said that it takes more muscles to frown than to smile. Let's learn to smile and laugh more. To enjoy our lives more. Yawns are contagious; I believe smiles can be, too. So smile today! Who knows? Your smile could even save someone's life.

What can you smile about today?

Don't Quit Before Your Miracle

By now your body is starting to change, and your mind also should be getting clearer and more focused. If you're starting to live by the principles set forth in this book, your life is getting better. Your marriage and career should be getting stronger.

Here's the problem: most people start to see changes taking place, but for one reason or another they don't continue on the path. They get started toward the life they want, but because this lifestyle change is new to them, they slip back into old habits, and the changes are short lived. We need a permanent lifestyle change, not a temporary change.

We need to remember where we came from and why we do not want to go back. Don't give up or give

Don't Quit Before Your Miracle

in; stay the course! Don't give up before your miracle comes into your life! Once it does come, let's help bring miracles into the lives of others.

It may feel like it's a miracle to achieve the life you want, but it's all in your hands. If you can dream it, you can achieve it!

What changes have you noticed in yourself in the last six weeks?

DAY 43
Don't Quit Before Your Miracle

What changes would you like to see in yourself in the next six weeks?

Don't Wait

There will never be a perfect moment to do something. It's always easier to come up with excuses. "I'm too tired to work out." "I will start after the holidays." "I can't afford to eat healthy." How many times do we say we're going to do something or that we could do this or that . . . *but*. We say we're going to do something, and then we follow it up with *but this* or *but that*. Our word is our bond. We are only as good as our word. If you live up to the promise you've made to others, that's great, and that's what should be done. But now it's time to keep your word when it comes to your promises to yourself.

Take the risk, make the jump—what do you have to lose? If you failed in the past, so what? What have you learned from your failures and how will you apply it to your life today?

There are really only three days that matter: yesterday, today, and tomorrow. Yesterday, because what you chose to do yesterday affects today. Today, because what you choose to do today will affect tomorrow.

Small, everyday choices add up. For example, each meal is a decision for or against our health. Each personal interaction is an opportunity to build up or break down ourselves and others. Each day the choice to work out or not is also a choice that is for or against our health.

We started this journey; now let's keep our word to ourselves. Let's make the right choices today so we have a brighter tomorrow.

A Day of Reflection

Congratulations, you've made it to the halfway point. You're doing great! Today is a day for reflecting back on the first part of your journey. Ask yourself the following questions, and rate yourself on how you have been doing.

How do you feel about where you are in your journey?

___
___
___
___
___
___

What are you working toward?

Where do you ultimately want to be?

DAY 45
A Day of Reflection

What do you want out of life?

What do you want more than anything right now in your life?

DAY 45
A Day of Reflection

What drives you?

Where do you get your motivation?

DAY 45
A Day of Reflection

Have you set defined, measurable goals?

If not, why not?

How are you going to reach your goals?

Are you rewarding yourself along the way?

DAY 45
A Day of Reflection

What's important to you today?

What are some steps you can take to have a better outcome in your life?

DAY 45
A Day of Reflection

What can you do to advance your career?

How has your marriage changed during this process?

DAY 45
A Day of Reflection

You're learning to manage your health, but are you learning to manage your debts?

Are you doing things to improve your life and the lives of your loved ones?

DAY 45
A Day of Reflection

Are you following through on your goals?

What's something new in your life?

DAY 45
A Day of Reflection

What changes have you seen in this first six weeks?

Have you tried something different or new in the last six weeks?

What are you proud of yourself for right now?

_____
_____
_____
_____
_____
_____
_____
_____
_____
_____

So, how did you do? If you are falling short in an area or two, then now is the time to adjust, take a look at your goals, realign yourself with what's important to you, and move forward.

Reward Yourself

Celebration day—you've made it over the halfway point. What can you do today to reward yourself?

We all like to be recognized and rewarded in our life. Go and do something that will put a smile on your face today. Buy yourself a new outfit or plan a weekend getaway with a friend or significant other. Maybe buy yourself some new workout equipment or take a cooking class. Whatever you choose, do something good for yourself.

Most people quit by this point. But you're not a quitter. You deserve more, and you are taking steps to get more out of your life. You keep doing the right things, and therefore the right things will come to you. I'm proud of you, and you should be proud of yourself.

It's important to recognize our achievements, be proud of ourselves, and reward ourselves for our hard work and discipline. You're doing a great job, and you deserve to recognize that in your life. No one else may know all that it's taken for you to get this far, but you know, and you should be very, very proud!

Therefore, take a day for yourself, and do something that will bring you joy. You deserve a reward today!

How will you reward yourself today?

Mold Your Life

Get over the thought that you're on a diet. This isn't a diet. This is a lifestyle change.

To this point, you may have been able to watch what you eat by restraining yourself. But if you haven't made an emotional change yet, you are likely to fail.

Your old self likes to creep up and take over. We need to figure out why we ate the way we did in the past. We need to learn to dig deep and find out what emotions have been driving us toward food. What makes us sell off our future for a little pleasure today?

Depression comes from living in the past. Anxiety comes from living in the future, not in the present. We can find hope, serenity, and peace by living in the present. You can look back on your past, but don't stare.

DAY 47
Mold Your Life

Life is what we make it through our actions. If you don't like the life you have, you can change it by changing your actions. Our actions determine our future.

Our creator gave us free will to choose our actions. We can choose life or choose death. Our creator wants you and me to choose life and have it more abundantly.

We need to quit being depressed over the past and anxious about the future. From this point on, will you waste your time wallowing and worrying, or will you invest your time wisely through positive action today?

What action can I take today that will mold my future into a more positive outcome?

Are You an Addict?

There are certain foods I know I can't have in the house. The sight of food triggers a sometimes overwhelming desire to put it in my mouth.

The problem is that one bite is one too many. Why do I say that? Because once I take one bite, it seems like a thousand bites are never enough. I go into an eating frenzy. If you're like me, an addict, then whatever your food triggers happen to be, you have to get them out of the house.

Certain types of food have strong effects on the body. Take sugar, for example. Our body wants more. It can never be satisfied. Whoever said a Snickers bar "satisfies" lied to us. It never satisfied me: it just left me wanting more.

As former addicts, we will always tend to have addictive tendencies. This is a battle we have to constantly fight.

I know this much: if I sit in a barbershop long enough, I'm going to get a haircut. If I sit in a bar long enough, odds are good I'll eventually have a drink. If I keep the foods I'm obsessing over in the house long enough, I'm probably going to eat them.

I'm trying to learn that nothing tastes as good as healthy feels, and foods that naturally go bad in a few days tend to be very healthy. They are clean-burning, high-energy fuel for the body.

I'm working from the philosophy "Out with the old and in with the new" when it comes to my eating habits. But why do I turn to so-called comfort foods, and why do you? I suggest that, deep down, something's broken; there's a sense of inadequacy.

We have to learn to love ourselves and treat ourselves as we treat others. We would probably never say to a friend that they are fat and ugly and undeserving—that they don't measure up and are losers. So why do we say these things to ourselves when we look in the mirror?

Scripture tells us to love our neighbor as ourselves. But if our words are kinder to our neighbors than to ourselves, we need to talk to ourselves differently. We should love ourselves as we love others.

DAY 48
Are You an Addict?

You were born to be a winner, and winners win. If you want to be successful, you need to design your life for success. Today would be a good day to organize the pantry and the refrigerator. Allow only good foods in your house.

Create a game plan for success, and you will succeed!

What's something you can get out of the house today to help you on this journey?

Are You an Addict?

Write a list of positive things about yourself and your surroundings, about what you have and the people in your life!

Turn Some Pages

As REO Speedwagon sang in their song "Keep on Rollin," "So if you're tired of the same old story, turn some pages. I will be here when you are ready to roll with the changes." I think both you and I are tired of the same old story. It is time to turn some pages.

We can do anything we set our minds to if we retrain our minds. The same old inputs, however, give only the same old outputs. If we want different outputs, we need different inputs.

There are great books and magazines devoted to the subject of training yourself to think differently, to find the positive in all situations. Podcasts are one of my favorite ways of reprogramming my mind. The

right podcast can help you avoid falling into negativity. I listen to them in the shower and in my car.

I'm working on making better use of my time because I'm tired of the same old story. This is one way I'm turning the pages. How will you turn the pages in your life to get the outcomes you desire?

What's one way you can "turn some pages" today?

Nothing New

If it seems that I'm saying the same thing only in different ways, you are correct. Sometimes it takes days, weeks, months, and maybe even years for something to sink in. We may hear the information a dozen or more times before something takes hold, before the seed finally sprouts.

An example of this is my favorite speaker, Zig Ziglar. I've recently started listening to the Ziglar podcast and implementing his philosophies into my daily life. These are not new philosophies. Most everything I hear, I've heard before. I just never totally jumped feet first into the deep end of the pool. Instead, I would slowly dip my toe in the water to make sure it's not too hot or too cold—not too much out of my comfort zone.

If something takes you a little out of your comfort zone, do you tentatively dip your toe into it or jump in feet first? In the past, I just dipped my toe when it came to the changes I needed to make in my life, and if I did jump in, a lot of times I jumped right back out. How about you?

Listening daily to inspiring podcasts is helping me jump in and stay in. Again, it's nothing new, but I'm uploading new ways of thinking into my mind daily, knowing that where the mind goes, the body will follow. One plus one is two, and A+B=C—these are the basics, and that's what this book focuses on. I want to focus on the basics daily until it becomes a part of me and a part of you.

My hope is that through repetition, our minds will be renewed every day, that we will jump in feet first, and that our goals will once and for all become our realities.

I'm jumping in. Will you?

What have you been too afraid to just jump into?

DAY 50
Nothing New

What can you do differently this time to jump all in?

Move to Lose

Your worst exercise day is far better than a day with no exercise. And today, getting good exercise is easier than ever.

There are great activity trackers out on the market that track everything for you, from total steps to calories burned. They include calories consumed and even sleep patterns. I recently bought the Jawbone Up2 for less than $100, and it's great. If I use it properly and track all my meals, I will know where I stand at the end of each day.

It's exciting to break previous days' records and start seeing changes in your life. I recently went nine miles on the treadmill. A new record! On day 19 I hit eight miles, which also happened to be a new high for me.

Don't think, however, that you have to go eight or nine miles to make a difference. That's not my typical day. Usually I will do one to three miles, two to three times a week, and it's working—the weight is coming off.

On rare occasions, I decide to really go for it. I have a goal to do a half marathon on the treadmill by day 91, even if I have to walk most of it. That's 13.1 miles. If you asked me a year ago how far a half marathon is, I would have had no idea. But now I'm going to go for it!

As your mind clears up with proper nutrition, exercise, and reading, watching, and listening to positive, uplifting messages, your interests may also change. In high school, you couldn't have given me a million dollars to run track. But nowadays I'm finding I enjoy it. My daughter and I even want to do some fun runs this spring and summer.

You can be a great example for your family. Maybe you can only go a block, but that's a start. The next day, try to go further. How about two blocks? Then the next day three blocks. You get the picture. Small improvements add up, and in time you will be breaking records and going farther than you ever thought possible.

As Neil Armstrong said, "That's one small step for man, one giant leap for mankind." Your daily effort is one small step for yourself, one giant leap for your heart, mind, and overall health!

DAY 51
Move to Lose

What is one goal you want to achieve by day 91?

What is a fun activity you can get your family involved in for a more active lifestyle?

Make It Fun

Yesterday we talked about moving to lose, and I left you with the question about an activity to get your family involved in to start moving more.

One thing my daughter and I do for fun is go to the tennis court and hit the ball around. I have to admit we are pretty bad; we don't even know the rules of the game. But the fun part is seeing how many times we can hit the ball back and forth without missing it. Even if it goes into another court we run and try to hit it back. All we care about is the number of hits back and forth, and then we start again and try to beat our high number. Not only do we have lots of fun and spend time together, but we also get in lots of steps. Since we are pretty bad, we are running all over the court. This is just one way to get moving more while making it fun.

It would also be fun to get the family together for a picnic and play a game of Whiffle ball, badminton, or volleyball. Get creative. When we learn to move more, we will easily lose more, and the more fun we make our activities, the more likely we will be to stick to it. Step out of your comfort zone, and give something new a try. I hope you find fun in some new activities today!

Accountability Partner

Who are you accountable to?

We are more likely to stick with the program when we are accountable to others. When people hold our feet to the fire, we tend to strive a little harder. Putting my name on this book makes me accountable to you, the reader; that's made me work harder to make the book as good as it can be.

Have you told anyone else your goals? You might want to consider hiring a trainer to hold you accountable. I've heard of people telling their friends their goals with the stipulation that if they didn't accomplish a goal, they would owe their friend a good amount of money. If we knew not hitting our goals might cost us something, I'd bet we'd be a little more accountable.

On *The Biggest Loser* the contestants weigh in weekly in front of one another. On *Extreme Weight Loss Makeover* Chris Powell has his clients weigh in every 90 days with the final weigh-in taking place in front of all their family and friends. This, again, helps to make them accountable to someone.

When we are accountable to others, it makes it a lot harder to blow off a workout. You and a friend could also take pictures of all your meals and snacks and text them to one another. If you both were honest, wouldn't this make you think for a second before you put that food into your mouth? If your friend cares about you, he would call you on the carpet when he receives pictures of cookies, ice cream, or pizza.

Accountability partners can help one another through the tough times and keep each other on track. That's why programs like Al-Anon and AA have as part of their programs finding someone to sponsor you. Sponsorship works! Being accountable to someone else can help strengthen you and help you quit falling short. Who are you accountable to, or who could you be accountable to today?

DAY 53

Accountability Partner

Make a list of people you respect who would hold you accountable on your journey. Work on getting one or more of them to commit to holding you accountable.

2.3 Ounces

Day 54 and I'm down approximately 18 pounds. That's a healthy weight loss of two to three pounds per week. But now that we are in week eight, what if I were down only seven, eight, or nine pounds? Would I quit, or would I continue on this journey?

Eight pounds in eight weeks might not seem like that much since it's only a pound a week. But it's a step forward, and when we are stepping forward, eventually we will reach the destination.

For example, a 300-pound person has a choice. He can lose a pound every week, or he can gain a pound every week. I know that doesn't seem like a whole lot, but in only two years that 300-pound person could now be 404 pounds, or that same 300-pound person could be 196 pounds, all just by gaining or losing a pound a week.

So maybe it takes you two years. That's OK if every week you're heading in the right direction. I know two years sounds like forever. Maybe you think you don't have two years to drop the weight; however, I bet you wish two years ago you would have started and stayed on this journey. Then you could say today that you weigh up to 104 pounds less than you did then.

Every day counts. Every day we have a choice. If we continue to move backwards, away from our goals, for the next two years, it may take four years to get back on track. You can either move toward or away from your goal.

Let me ask you: If you really, really wanted to gain 2.3 ounces today, could you? How about tomorrow? What about the next day?

Could you gain a pound this week by gaining only 2.3 ounces a day if you really set your mind to it? Yes? Well, that tells me that if your mind was set on gaining 2.3 ounces today, then you could just as easily lose 2.3 ounces today if you set your mind to it.

That would be a healthy weight loss of one pound per week. In two years you could have shed as much as 104 pounds from your current weight, all by losing just 2.3 ounces per day.

2.3 Ounces

It's your choice. You can choose a healthy lifestyle or choose the bondage that the weight brings into your life. Which will you choose?

Maybe you don't need to lose a total of a 104 pounds, or maybe you need to lose more. Maybe so far you have lost only seven or eight pounds in this process. So what? Don't be discouraged. You're on your way and are moving forward, toward your goal.

Picture in your mind what your life would look like today if you had started this journey two years ago. What if you were at your ideal weight? How would you look? How would you feel? What effects would that have on your lifestyle and your family today?

You Are Where You Are

My favorite speaker and author, Zig Ziglar, used to say something like, "You are what you are and you are where you are because of what has gone into your mind. You change what you are and you change where you are by changing what goes into your mind." This is a true statement and the whole idea behind this book.

To piggyback off of the famous Zig Ziglar quote, "You look and feel the way you do by what has gone into your mouth. You can change the way you look and you can change the way you feel by changing what goes into your mouth."

We need to realize that food is not therapy. I know a lot of us tend to eat more when we are sad, depressed, or angry. Food has become a crutch for us.

DAY 55
You Are Where You Are

What we have put into our mouth has affected us and where we are in our life. When we change what we put into our mouth by choosing a healthier alternative, our bodies will change, and our minds will become clear. You've heard the saying that an apple a day keeps the doctor away. I don't know if this is true or not, but I do know a chocolate bar a day doesn't keep the weight away.

We have to quit trading what we want most for what we want right now. When you look at a piece of food today, ask yourself, "Is this going to bring me closer to or push me farther away from my ultimate goal?" Life is a series of choices, and eventually they add up to a good or bad outcome.

What outcome will you strive for?

The next time you're mad, sad, or depressed, what's something different you could do to avoid seeking comfort in food?

_____
_____
_____
_____
_____

DAY 55
You Are Where You Are

The Reward

Do you reward yourself properly?

Here's how I used to reward myself. I'd allow myself to eat anything and everything I wanted for having a good week. Oftentimes I would start on Monday with the mindset that if I had done well during the week—meaning, I'd made good meal choices—my reward would be bad food choices on the weekend. All to start again on Monday.

I was living for the weekend and was not focused on the long-term results. My reward was working against my goals. How crazy is that?

If your child got straight A's one semester, would your reward be to allow him or her to slack off and bring home all F's the next semester? Of course not. So why do we reward ourselves counterproductively?

There may be times that we are just going to get an F. Maybe we didn't prepare for a situation. That's fine. We learn to bounce back. But to purposely earn a bunch of F's just doesn't work.

Lets quit rewarding ourselves with F's and stay on the Honor Roll today.

What are some counterproductive rewards you've given yourself in the past?

_____
_____
_____
_____
_____
_____
_____
_____
_____
_____
_____
_____
_____

DAY 56
The Reward

What would be a more appropriate reward for a job well done?

Past Mistakes

Have you made mistakes in the past? Sure you have. Who hasn't?

Leaders learn not to let mistakes control their life. They learn from their mistakes and try not to repeat them.

The real problem with mistakes isn't that others won't forgive and forget them. It's we who oftentimes won't. It's easier to forgive others than forgive ourselves.

We let our mistakes eat us up. We let them define us. Instead of learning and moving on, we often let a mistake control us.

We have to realize that a mistake was just an event that happened. It's an opportunity for learning and growing. A mistake is not us personally. We are not a mistake. God doesn't make mistakes; therefore, you are not one.

Let's quit defining ourselves by our standards and start defining ourselves by God's standards. God sees us justified and redeemed, forgiven and sanctified, victorious and more than conquerors, the very apple of his eye. He loved us so much he gave His only begotten Son to take on the death penalty our sins deserve.

God Himself doesn't see us in terms of our mistakes. So how much longer will you see yourself that way?

What's a past mistake you have held onto that has had a negative impact on your life?

DAY 57
Past Mistakes

What is something you can learn from a past mistake, and what's something you can do to move past that mistake, to realize it's just an event, not you as a person?

What's Right?

Stop harping on what's wrong with you, and give yourself a boost by looking at what's right. You have marvelous, unique qualities.

Sometimes in our lives, we get stuck in a rut. The reason we can't seem to get out of the rut usually boils down to negative self-talk. We like to criticize our looks, talents, careers, and overall life situations.

You've probably heard the definition of insanity: "doing the same thing over and over again but expecting different results." The results don't change until we change. It's just that simple.

You may not think you have the ability to change. But do you have heart? That is where your power to change resides.

Heart will outperform talent every time. And as you put your heart into change, talent will surface. When you have heart, you will no longer want to waste your time but rather will find ways to invest your time wisely.

For example, at this very moment, as I'm writing this, I just dropped my daughter off for a ninety-minute piano practice. My old self would have just driven around and killed time—maybe have even grabbed some fast food. But today I'm investing my time into writing this book while I sit in the parking lot. My old self would have wasted ninety minutes instead of investing it.

We all have the same twenty-four hours each day. What will you choose to do with the precious time you've been given? There really are only two choices: waste it or invest it. What will you choose?

In the past, how have you wasted your time instead of investing it?

_____

_____

_____

_____

_____

DAY 58
What's Right?

How can you better invest your time?

59

Living Outside Your Comfort Zone

If you want something you've never had, you have to do something you've never done. You have to step out on a limb. Get out of your comfort zone. It's time to take action.

Every action matters. It matters to you and to your family and friends. And it matters even to me. Our actions shape the world around us, and I want my children and grandchildren to grow up in a better world.

Speaking of venturing outside of our comfort zones, I'm taking my own advice. At the end of this month, I'm taking a two-day class held by the Ziglar Corporation on essential presentation skills. It's about speaking in public. To be truthfully honest, I'm scared to death. This is outside of my comfort zone. I've always been more of an introvert. From what I understand, by the end of the second day, we will give a presentation in front of a group and be taped for evaluation.

Again totally nervous about this, but if we want to be great, we have to go out on that limb. We have to step out in faith and have the courage to move forward.

I know that as I change my world, I can have an impact on this world. But it starts with me. I have to change myself before I can change others.

Will you go out on a limb, too?

What's something that in the past you would have never been willing to do but are now willing to give a shot?

DAY 59

Living Outside Your Comfort Zone

How will you follow through?

Another Day of Reflection

Congratulations! You've made it through month two. You're two-thirds of the way done. But remember: this isn't just a ninety-one day program; this is meant to be a lifestyle.

I hope the changes you have made will stay with you today, tomorrow, and the rest of your life. Let's have another day of reflection to see how you're doing up to this point.

How have you done for your first sixty days?

_____
_____
_____

What are you excited about right now in your life as you move forward?

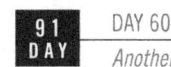

DAY 60

Another Day of Reflection

Joseph Abney

What struggles have you endured and overcome in these sixty days?

How much weight have you lost in your first sixty days?

DAY 60

Another Day of Reflection

Take the number above and multiply it by six. What is that number?

Now take that number and subtract it from your beginning weight. This will show you where you could possibly be in ten more months. What is that number?

If it took you 365 days to get to that number, will it be worth it and why?

DAY 60
Another Day of Reflection

Whatever that number is, you are so much more than a number. What great traits do you possess?

What about yourself are you most proud of today?

DAY 60
Another Day of Reflection

Other than the weight loss, what are some other positive things you have noticed in the last sixty days?

_____
_____
_____
_____
_____
_____
_____
_____
_____
_____
_____
_____

Congratulations on your first sixty days into this journey. I'm excited for both you and me on our new lifestyle. I pray that life gives you everything you want and that you find passion every day!

React or Respond?

Life happens. Often when things seem to be going well, life will drop a bomb on us. This is when we run to unhealthy foods, drugs, or alcohol for comfort.

Anytime bad things happen or situations out of our control come our way, we have a choice. We can either react or respond. To react is negative. We are letting ourselves be controlled by circumstances outside our control.

But when we *respond* to these situations, we often find solutions. We conquer the situation. This is how we learn. This is how we grow.

To respond is positive. Some people let situations drag them down, while others overcome and are lifted up. This develops our character. Do you want to be an overcomer and the type of person people look up to and admire, or do you want to be overcome and envy others, thinking they have it so easy? The truth is they have the same problems, situations, and temptations as everybody else. The difference is they just choose to respond and look for a solution to overcome the obstacles set before them.

To react or to respond is a choice we all get to make. Which one we choose develops our character.

Next time life throws you a bomb, which will you choose?

Name a time in your life that you reacted to a situation.

How did that turn out for you?

Name a time that you chose to respond to a situation.

What was the benefit of responding instead of reacting?

Self-Talk

We all need a little positive self-talk daily. For most of our lives, we hear nothing but negativity and how we can't accomplish much of anything. Well, today is the day to start talking to yourself in a more positive manner. Positive in = Positive out.

You can get the following self-talk cards from www.Ziglar.com/selftalk. These are Zig Ziglar's self-talk cards, meant to be read out loud first thing in the morning and last thing before bed. Do this for the rest of your ninety-one days, and I guarantee you will see results. Here they are:

Every morning before you start your day and every evening at the close of the day, stand in front of the mirror in a room by yourself, look yourself in

the eyes (the eyes are the window to the soul), and say: I _____ am a child of the king (John 1:12) **in the will of God** (The Lord's Prayer) **and can do all things through Christ who gives me strength** (Philippians 4:13). **I claim the following attributes because I have the mind of Christ** (1 Corinthians 2:11), **am a confidant of God** (Psalms 25:14) **and although I am weak in many of these qualities I am specifically told** (Joel 3:10) **to let the weak say I am strong. By claiming, developing and using these Biblical qualities, I will become the person God created me to be and will glorify God and benefit mankind.**

> A) **I _____ am an honest, intelligent, organized, responsible, committed, teachable person who is sober, loyal, and clearly understands that regardless of who signs my paycheck I am self-employed. I am an optimistic, punctual, enthusiastic, goal-setting smart working self-starter who is a disciplined, focused, dependable, persistent positive thinker with great self-control, and am an energetic and diligent team player and hard worker who appreciates the opportunity my company and the free-enterprise system offer me. I am thrifty with my resources and**

DAY 62
Self-Talk

apply common sense to my daily tasks. I take honest pride in my competence, appearance and manners, and am motivated to do my best so that my healthy self-image will remain on solid ground. These are the qualities which enable me to manage myself and help give me employment security in a no-job-security world.

B) I, _____, am a compassionate, respectful encourager who is considerate, generous, gentle, patient, caring, sensitive, personable, attentive, fun-loving person. I am a supportive, giving and forgiving, clean, kind, unselfish, affectionate, loving, family-oriented, human being, and I am a sincere and open-minded good listener and a good-finder who is trustworthy. These are the qualities which enable me to build good relationships with my associates, neighbors, mate and family.

C) I _____, am a person with integrity! With the faith and wisdom to know what I should do and the courage and convictions to follow through. I have the vision to manage myself and to lead others. I am authoritative, confident, and humbly grateful for the opportunity life offers me. I am fair, flexible, resourceful, creative, knowledgeable, decisive, and an extra-miler with a servant's attitude who communicates well with others. I am a consistent, pragmatic teacher with character and a finely tuned sense of humor. I am an honorable person and am balanced in my personal, family and business life, and have a passion for being, doing and learning more today so I can be, do and have more tomorrow.

D) These are the qualities of a winner I was born to be, and I am fully committed to developing these marvelous qualities with which I have been entrusted. Tonight I'm going to sleep wonderfully well. I will dream powerful, positive dreams. I will awaken energized and refreshed; tomorrow's going to be magnificent and my future is unlimited. Recognizing, claiming and developing these qualities which I already have gives me a legitimate chance to be happier, healthier, more prosperous, more secure, have more friends, greater peace of mind, better family

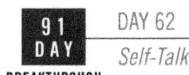

relationships and legitimate hope that the future will be even better.

Repeat the process the next morning and close by saying, "These are the qualities of the winner I was born to be and I will develop and use these qualities to achieve my worthy objectives. Today is a brand new day and it's mine to use in a marvelously productive way."

Wow! We all have these qualities within us. Now its time to remind ourselves every day.

Homework: Go to www.ziglar.com/selftalk and print out the "self-talk cards." Then begin the process of reading them out loud every morning and evening.

Self-Talk (Part 2)

Yesterday we discussed the self-talk cards. When I first started saying these out loud, I felt a little weird. In the past, I would say all kinds of negative things out loud, like, "Man, I'm getting fat" or "That was so stupid of me." Why do we so easily accept negative talk into our life but think it's weird to talk to ourselves in a positive manner?

At this moment, even if you don't feel like you have the qualities in the self-talk cards, know that you do have them. We all have these seeds of greatness; it's just that some of us have let them lie dormant for too long.

Reading these self-talk cards out loud every day is like pouring living water on dormant seeds. Those seeds will start to sprout and grow.

Stepping out of your comfort zone will lead you in the direction of greatness. We don't have to be great to start. Our nutrition plan might not be spot on. Our workouts may be weak. We may be filled with self-doubt and a limiting mindset. That's why we're on this journey—to learn to change our mindset.

Again, we don't have to be great to start, but we do have to start if we are ever to be great. Greatness begins with that leap of faith.

Step out and step up in your life. Let the seeds of greatness sprout forth!

What is a trait you have let lie dormant for too long?

_____
_____
_____
_____
_____
_____

Path of Decision

We have come to a crossroads in our life. We can choose to better ourselves or not.

What we often do, though, is choose the path of least resistance. We say to ourselves that the pathway to success is just too hard or that it's more than we can handle.

But what often happens as we travel down the path of least resistance is that we end up looking back with regrets. We thought the successful path would be tough, and now we realize that the tough thing is to live a life full of regrets, wishing we would have or knowing we should have.

Having traveled so far down the path of least resistance, we often tell ourselves it's too late to go back or to start over. But that's not true: you can always start again. We have that choice every day. We may not be able to fix all of our past mistakes, but we don't have to continue in them. We can change!

We don't have to wait; waiting got us to where we are. How much longer will we wait to change? Let's get on the path to our dreams, and as we walk down it, we ought to extend our hand to those who currently are where we once were.

Our weak will got us to where we were. Let's learn to turn our will over to God and ask Him to lead us down the right path this time. Try asking Him to remove food addictions just for today. The Bible says we have not because we ask not. Do your part, and I believe God will make up the difference.

Today, let's push through like never before, and when that path of decision comes our way, let us take the high road, not the low road.

DAY 64
Path of Decision

What else could you ask God to help you with today?

The A-Life

If you don't make things happen, things are still going to happen. That's life.

We can make our health great, or we can let our lifestyle control our health. We can make our marriage great, or we can just have a marriage. Our jobs can be everything we ever wanted, or they can just be jobs.

Life is so short. Today I want you to look at where you are failing in life and ask yourself, "Why? What can I do differently to quit failing?"

At this point, there may be areas you are getting an "F" in. Most people don't go from failing to being a straight-A student overnight. But they are capable of getting all A's.

If you have an "F" in a certain area of your life, get that grade up to a "D." It doesn't take a lot to move it a little bit. From there, go for a "C." Before long, you will be getting "B's," and then you'll be on your way toward building that straight-A life you have been dreaming about.

We've already discussed how "inch by inch, it's a cinch." Little steps in the right direction become big strides. Remember the turtle? He wins the race!

Now that you're on the right path, move forward. Pass the test, and better grades will come your way. Better grades = Better life.

The past semester is in the past. Today, class is in session. Now the only question that remains is, "Will you show up today?"

What is an area in your life you believe you are failing in?

_____
_____
_____
_____
_____
_____

What can you do today to start getting your grades up in that area?

Day 66

Attitude of Gratitude

An attitude of gratitude is the best attitude one can have.

I'm thankful today for those who have guided me along life's way. Some people have helped me to see what I don't want to be. Others helped me to be what I want to be. I'm grateful to those who taught me the art of selling and to those who helped me through rough times in my life.

One of the things I'm most grateful for in my life is my family. My family loves me, and I love them. I'm thankful for my father-in-law. He's an example of what a healthy lifestyle can do. At the age of seventy, he did seventy pullups for his birthday. Wow! I'm lucky to do one. I look to him as my model of the condition I would like to be in when I'm seventy.

I'm thankful for the teachers who taught me and for the jobs I've had. From sweeping floors at a fast-food restaurant to manufacturing car parts to selling products face to face with clients, I wouldn't change a thing.

Life is a matter of choices—some good, some bad. Even the wrong choices, however, have shaped and molded me into who I am today.

I'm thankful for the free will God gave me to make my own decisions, from right decisions that have blessed me to wrong decisions that I have learned from. Today, I'm grateful for the very air that I breathe. We can always find the wrong in any situation, but if you look hard enough, you can and will find the good.

These are just a handful of what I'm grateful for in my life. How about you?

What are some things that have molded you into who you are today?

_____

_____
_____
_____
_____

DAY 66
Attitude of Gratitude

How or why are you grateful about these things that have molded you into who you are today?

"Drained"

Sometimes you have to pause or make a brief stop to refill the tank. If you just get in your car and go and never stop to refuel, eventually you're going to run out of gas. When we run out of gas, we stall.

That's what the self-talk cards we discussed on day 62 are all about: taking that time out for yourself and reminding yourself just who you are. It's the same with reading a good book or listening to a self-help podcast. It's putting gas in the car.

When your tank is full, you can spare a little gas to help others, but if the gauge is on "E," what do you have to give?

A pause actually helps us continue forward, to move down the road. You will not reach that destination until you work these purposeful pauses into your life. Your tank will become empty, and you will stall. And sometimes the tow truck driver's fee to get you up and running again can be expensive.

A pause here or there will keep you on your way. With a full tank, you will, one day, reach your destination!

What are we waiting for? Let's hit the road!

What is a purposeful pause you could take to help you reach your destination?

_____
_____
_____
_____
_____
_____
_____
_____
_____
_____
_____

Determination of a Child

What if we could develop the determination of a child?

Isn't it something how children tend to get what they ask for? Sure, we may tell them no, maybe over and over again, and we may even mean it. But do you know what they hear when we say "no"? They don't hear "no," they hear "know"! They believe "no" doesn't really mean "no." They believe that we really just need to know more. So what do they do? They ask again. They get even more determined to get what they want.

What happens if we say "no" again? They may wait a day or two, but somehow it comes up again in conversation. You can bet they are going to get their way one way or another.

Well, what about us? Are we as determined as a child to get our way? They are extraordinarily persistent. You and I could learn from this. My children have me wrapped around their finger, and they are usually going to get what they want as long as it won't harm them, because I love them. But we have to love ourselves, too!

Are we going to get what we want? Will we be as determined as our children are? Guess what? We can indeed be just as determined. This is a trait our children have learned to develop, and if they can develop determination for something they really want, then so can we.

What do you want? Are you determined to get it? Our children can teach us amazing things. Isn't it time to humble ourselves and become as determined as a child to get what we really want?

Determination will get us there. Don't let the naysayers steal your determination.

Just Getting By

Getting by was something I had become accustomed to. I grew up in a little town called Viburnum. More than likely, you never heard of it. It has a population of around 700 people. If you blink while driving through, you're likely to miss it.

I believe there were 53 students in my graduating class. Guess where I was ranked out of the 53? I certainly was not in the top 10 percent or even in the top 20. OK, so not even in the top 50 percent. I think I was number 47 out of 53. I was right around the bottom 10 percent.

But I graduated. As a matter of fact, I prided myself on the fact that I never got an "F." Sure, I got an occasional

DAY 69

Just Getting By

"F" on tests and assignments but not on the report cards. That's all that really mattered to me. I always squeaked out "C's" and "D's"—just enough to get by.

How about you? Do you do just enough in certain areas of your life to just get by? Now that I'm in my 40s, I realize I still have the same tendency in certain areas of my life—to just get by. I could choose to do better, but getting by seemed to work for me. At least that's what I thought.

Also in my 40s, I prided myself on not taking any medicine. Even when a doctor would try to put me on something, I just refused to take it. I didn't want medicine for my health, but at the same time I did nothing but eat things to hurt my body. I was, again, just getting by.

Any new doctor I went to who asked what kind of medicine I was on was always shocked to find that I took no medicine because everybody seems to be on something. This reinforced my pride.

In reality, though, I was priding myself on a "C" and "D" life. Sure, I was on no medicine, but I was tired all the time. Depression ruled my days. My joy seemed to be diminished year by year. My weight kept increasing, and my goals and dreams seemed to get further and further away. Sure, I was living, but I wasn't truly LIVING!

DAY 69

Just Getting By

Now I'm learning to live a life with power. I'm learning to take better care of my body. I'm exchanging my "C" and "D" lifestyle for "A's" and "B's." Not every day will be an "A" day, but one thing's for sure: I'm no longer just getting by.

What areas of your life would you currently grade as "C" or "D" areas?

How can you start to increase your grades in those areas?

Keep the Fire Burning

As your transformation continues, some people may try to put out your fire.

We know that hurting people tend to hurt people. Not everybody will be as excited about the changes in your life as you are. Don't let them throw water on your fire.

We need to add daily fuel to the fire we have started. That daily fuel is what you decide to put into your mind on a daily basis.

Let's face it: we are surrounded with negative people. Negativity is everywhere. But guess what? Fire spreads; if we can start a fire and keep it going, we won't let people put our fire out with their negativity. If we keep adding fuel to the fire, it will spread. Maybe not everybody you come across will have their own flame ignited, but some will. And, in turn, their fire will spread to others.

With your positive attitude, you can bring change to this world. Only twelve disciples spread the good news of the Messiah to the whole world. The fire spread, and some caught it while others tried to put it out.

Your fire will spread and can affect millions. Just keep it burning!

When was a time you were excited about something going on in your life and someone threw water on your fire?

DAY 70
Keep the Fire Burning

The next time someone tries to put out your fire, how will you respond?

Balance

Balance is something we can benefit from.

Sometimes it's hard to squeeze everything we'd like to accomplish into twenty-four hours. I've struggled with balance in my life at times. Sometimes I get excited about my career, and my balance shifts toward that and away from my family. At other times, my balance is shifted toward my family, and my career suffers. And still other times, I get excited about something all together different, and then both career *and* family get neglected.

Balance is something worth working toward. If we are successful in our career but lose our family, we aren't successful. If we fail in our spirituality while succeeding elsewhere, then, again, we aren't truly successful. If most areas seem to be going well in our life but we are neglecting ourselves and our needs, our success will be short term and will crumble.

When we can find balance in all areas of our life, we will find success. If you want to keep the weight off this time, then this journey can't be about the weight only. It has to cross over into other areas of our life.

We need to have a healthy balance in all domains of our lives. When you're balanced, you're in control, and then you can accomplish your goals.

Almost nothing is out of reach for those walking in balance, because they know they are ultimately the ones responsible for their success or failure.

If there is an area you know is out of balance, start to work on that area today, and you'll see the great rewards that come from a balanced life.

What is an area of your life that is out of balance, and what are you willing to do to fix it?

DAY 71
Balance

Loyalty

I love my golden retriever. That breed is the most loyal, I believe. She has great traits. She wants to spend time with me. She always wants to shake my hand. She always has a smile on her face and a playful spirit.

I can count on her to bring me pleasure and happiness. If she does something wrong, she shows true remorse. She wants to be your friend even when she knows she is in trouble, and she will show you her sad little face until you are friendly to her again. If I don't give her enough attention, she will bark until I do. She is nothing but joyful at seeing me when I've been gone all day.

If only I could learn to have the love, joy, and happiness, the playful spirit, the loyalty my dog has for me, my world and the world around me would be so much better because I would always make those around me feel happy, too. If I could learn to embrace my new lifestyle as my golden retriever embraces me, change would be easy.

You never know where inspiration may come from. I'm inspired today to be more loyal to my new lifestyle and more loyal to others around me. As my golden retriever has inspired me, I will look to inspire others today, too.

What If

What if all of a sudden you couldn't see anymore? How tragic would that be?

More than likely, though, you can see and can choose what to focus on. You can focus on the beauty of the world or the corruption of the world.

What if all of a sudden you couldn't hear anymore? Again, how tragic that would be? Hopefully you can hear, though. You also have a choice of what to listen to. Do you listen to stories about the great things going on in the world or to stories of all the tragedies of the world?

What if all of a sudden you woke up and you couldn't speak? Again, hopefully, you can actually speak. You get to choose whether to speak life into others or to speak hurt and harm into them.

If you get to see, hear, and speak, you are blessed and can focus these gifts toward the negative or the positive. Don't neglect these gifts.

Will we use our senses and all our gifts to sit on the couch with a Big Mac, or will we use them to keep ourselves healthy and live up to our potential?

Just as our eyes get to focus on beauty or ugliness, just as our ears get to listen to stories of greatness or tragedy, just as our mouth gets to speak words of hurt or words of life, we get the same choice with our health. Junk food and a couch or movement and healthy food choices: you get to choose.

Isn't it time to focus on what we really want?

Time

How much time do you need to succeed?

Twenty-four hours is plenty of time. A lot of people say there just aren't enough hours in the day to accomplish what they want to accomplish. What if you had only twenty hours in a day? Twenty-four hours would start looking pretty good, wouldn't it?

You don't need more time; what you need is discipline and organization. Without these, it wouldn't matter if you had twenty-eight hours in a day. It still wouldn't be enough time.

A supposed lack of time to accomplish our goals is just another excuse. When will we stop looking at the obstacles and start asking ourselves what we can do to be successful?

If you're looking for an excuse, you don't have to look very far. There is always a reason to fail. When will you decide once and for all that failure is no longer an option? When you do, there is nothing that can hold you back.

What is an excuse you are going to throw out the window and never use again?

How will making this decision empower you?

Failure?

It's day 75. Have I failed in the first 75 days? Yes, I have. There have been days I didn't work out. There have been days I didn't plan out my meals and ate badly.

We talked on day 8 about the difference between slipping and sliding. In the last 75 days, there have been times I have definitely slipped. Old habits are hard to break.

One slip even started to turn into a big-time slide as I abandoned my good eating habits for three straight days. In the past, there would have been no recovery, but today is different. I caught myself and moved forward.

Why was I able to recover and get back on track? Because of the lessons in this book I have incorporated into my daily life. These lessons can do the same for you. Have you been keeping up with the self-talk cards? Are you listening to positive messages while you are driving? Are you taking quality time for yourself? And have you stepped outside your comfort zone and tried something new? These are a few things that have made a change in my life.

So yes, I have failed but pushed through and eventually succeeded. I've learned from my failures and at times may have lost the battle—but not the war.

If you have had temporary setbacks, that's not surprising; we all do. But how you handle these temporary failures will determine whether you will be successful or not.

Even though there have been some failures in the last 75 days, I'm way ahead of where I started and accomplishing things I would have never imagined possible. I've pulled out of the rut, and even though there may be a few bumps in the road, the rut is behind me.

So, ultimately, have I failed or succeeded? What about you?

DAY 75
Failure?

What have been some temporary setbacks you've come across in the last 75 days?

What have been some breakthroughs you have had since you started this journey?

Breakthrough

I had a goal that, before the 91 days in this book were up, I would run a half marathon. That's 13.1 miles, a distance I'd never run in my life. Today was that day. I got on the treadmill and decided to go for it. Almost three hours later, I hit the goal.

Our bodies are so much more capable than we give them credit for. We can accomplish amazing feats.

It's funny how your mind tries to stop you. During the three hours, a little voice kept popping up in my head telling me things like, "Haven't you done enough?" "This is crazy—why don't you quit?" "This doesn't prove anything. Why do you want to do this, anyway?" "You know that running a half marathon outdoors would be the real test; the treadmill is the wimpy way to do this."

We all have to learn to turn off that voice inside our head saying "I can't" and turn on the one that says "I can."

To complete the half marathon was nice, but the real victory was shutting down the voice of self-defeat and finishing what I started.

I hope this will help you break through today.

Today's Challenge:

Set a goal of something you would like to accomplish by day 91—make it something that would be a real breakthrough for you.

Partly or Fully Committed

I'm not where I want to be, but I'm not where I once was. Perfection takes time. A work of art is something you work toward.

With my first 91 days almost complete, I'm heading in the right direction. I would estimate that, with two more rounds of equally good progress, I will be where I would like to be. Not bad for getting back to a healthy stage in just nine months—considering I've been heading in the other direction for more than twenty years.

I could have made the same choice years ago, but I didn't. I could have decided to gain my confidence, strength, health, and joy back, but instead I let my mind tell my body that it just was too tough. I also let food control me instead of learning to control food.

The time to get healthy is now! The time has always been right now; I just didn't make the choice. I only committed part way in the past, and that's why it never worked. My part-way commitment caused me to waste twenty years of my life. A part-way desire to accomplish your goals will never get you to the finish line.

That finish line may seem so far off as to be unreachable, but with a full commitment, you go as far as you can see, and then you will be able to see farther. As you run around the track of life, you might not see the finish line; you might only be able to see the curve ahead. But once you get around the curve, you will see the next section of the track and how to navigate that area clearly until, one day, you will see the finish line and know how to reach it.

This time, let's not just partly commit. Let's fully commit, which means these ninety-one days are not the end but only the beginning of a new, better you!

DAY 77

Partly or Fully Committed

What are you going to do on day 91 to keep yourself moving full-steam ahead and not backward into old patterns?

Lights, Camera, Action!

No action = No positive outcome.

If you want to be in the limelight, if you want to feel camera worthy, then take action right now, because if you wait till tomorrow, tomorrow will never come.

You will regret it at some point if you don't take action now. You have nothing to lose and everything to gain by going for it.

Is it going to hurt to take action? Yes! You're going to go through pain—either the initial pain of doing something or the pain of regret. However, the initial pain goes away as you get stronger, whereas the pain of regret usually stays with us.

It's time to quit cheating the person in the mirror. You're worth the effort. Others achieve their dreams, so why not you? If you dream it, you can achieve it.

If you haven't already, it's time to write out your goals and have an action plan for reaching them. When you put forth the effort, then and only then will you get to the positive outcome you desire.

Choose to take the appropriate action in your life, and, as you do, this world might just say to you: "Lights, Camera, Action! You've become a star!"

If you took action now, what kind of pain might you experience?

DAY 78

Lights, Camera, Action!

How painful will it be if you choose not to take action, and what might that cost you in the long run?

Not Another Excuse

It's so easy to find a reason not to do what you know you should do. Every morning, it is so easy for me to get caught up in daily life. When that happens, I often put off the important things that I know I should be doing to accomplish my goals. We often don't take the time we need for ourselves, whether it's in our spiritual pursuits, like taking the time for prayer and bible study, or our physical pursuits, like exercise and proper nutrition. We get in a hurry to get things done, with little conscious effort on taking the time to become the best that we can be. There's always a reason to put off what you know you should be doing, however, when we continue to put off what we know we should be doing, then, eventually, we have to face the consequence of that. This could be manifested in poor health, marriages, our spirituality, and even our careers. We are all given the same 24 hours in a day. Will we learn to control the day through proper planning and action, or will we continue to let the day control us and slip away as we keep sliding farther from our goals? Today I want you to break through the excuses that have kept you captive in the past and do what you know you should be doing to reach your goals. When you plan and prepare to win, then you are one step closer to the goal that you have set out to achieve.

What is a limiting excuse you have made in the past?

How can you plan and prepare to win today?

Action Inspires

There will be times in your life when you are just not inspired. When this happens, we can still choose to push through and break down that barrier.

When we choose to do this, we in turn become inspired. Action is what breeds inspiration. Others can inspire us, but until we take action ourselves, that inspiration will be short lived.

An example of temporary inspiration with no fundamental change would be watching a weight-loss transformation on TV. You may be totally inspired and know that if those people can accomplish what they did, then so could you. But until you actually take action and find your own inspiration within, you're left with an unfulfilled dream once the show's over.

We have to conquer procrastination. Procrastination breeds and multiplies. For example, I know what I need to eat today as part of my plan to reach my goals. If I choose to eat the wrong things today, will sticking to the plan tomorrow be any easier? No. It will probably be harder.

When you put off doing what you know you should do, it gets easier and easier to continue with old, destructive behaviors. If this were not true, then neither you nor I would have a problem with our weight. The reason we do is because we have put something off we know we should be doing.

Big "Yes" to listening to or watching inspirational programs. But big Double Yes to becoming inspired through your actions. If you can put both together, you're a Triple Threat. Nothing can stand in your way!

Next time you are totally uninspired, what will you do?

_____
_____
_____
_____
_____
_____
_____

Unleash Your Greatness

You have greatness inside you, but you will never see the greatness until you decide to unleash it.

That's right, you have to decide. No one else can do it for you. You may be in a routine of doing the right things when it comes to health and attaining your other goals, but are you committed?

There's a big difference. A routine is just a series of things you may be doing on a regular basis, but it may have not become a "have to" yet.

It's time to get committed, once and for all. When you finally decide to make the commitment, then and only then will you start to see the greatness unleash itself.

Commitment is like making sure the fire is burning and will continue to burn. You have struck a match with the things you've done so far, but will you use that match to light the larger fire, or will you let it burn out? Are you just in a routine that may fade away, or are you full-on committed?

When you're committed, it's no longer "I would like to make a change" but "I'm *going* to make a change." When you commit, goals become a reality. You accomplish great things because you are committed to the process; you're not just hanging out.

Unleash your greatness by getting totally committed today. You'll be glad you did!

What's a commitment you can make to yourself that will move you closer to where you want to be?

_____
_____
_____
_____
_____
_____
_____
_____
_____
_____

Love Yourself

If you could make a living out of loving yourself, would you be a millionaire, or would you be poor?

It's so important to love yourself and build a good healthy self-image. Why are we so often our worst critic? God loves us, faults and all. He loves us so much that He gave His only begotten Son to die on the cross for us. If He loves us this much, why can't we seem to overlook our faults?

The tendency to be critical of ourselves can spill over onto others, like family and friends. Even if we are not directly critical of family, our habit of criticizing ourselves is often adopted by our children. If our children hear us say, "I'm fat" or "Nothing good ever happens to me," they will begin to see themselves in the same light.

Our words are powerful! What if our family heard us accepting ourselves with positive affirmations, with words of love? What if they knew we accepted ourselves and loved ourselves, faults and all? Would we not also be able to love others despite their faults?

Galatians 5: 23-24 says that the fruit of the Spirit starts with love, and then come joy, peace, longsuffering, gentleness, goodness, faith, meekness, and temperance. You can't have the others without the first one—love.

How much joy will you have if you don't have love? Without love, we won't have much peace. Learn to love yourself and develop a healthy self-image. Learn not just to love yourself, but love God and grow in the fruits of the Spirit. You will become the person you were destined to be!

Do you manifest the fruit of the Spirit or rotten fruit in your day-to-day activities?

_____

_____

_____

_____

DAY 82

Love Yourself

If you are manifesting rotten fruit, what will you do to change your life?

Prepare

When we prepare our mind and body, we prepare our future. When we have no plan and make no preparation for getting to where we want to be, we are planning to fail.

A ship will never reach its destination unless it has its course mapped out. When we plan and prepare, we are mapping our course for a better future. On the other hand, if we're just coasting, we're living life on life's terms, not our own.

We can determine whether we will be successful or not in our life. In every one of life's spheres, we have that choice: our marriages, our careers, with our overall weight and health. When we don't plan in these areas, they start to deteriorate.

DAY 83
Prepare

Whenever we have failed, it isn't because we wanted to. We just didn't plan and prepare. Sure, life happens, and we play the cards we are dealt. But when you plan and prepare, you become the dealer, and you control the hand that you are dealt.

So take a minute and make sure to plan for success today.

What is something you have planned for and prepared for in the last eighty-three days, and what progress has come out of that planning and preparation?

_____
_____
_____
_____
_____
_____
_____
_____
_____
_____
_____
_____

Can-Do Attitude

We need to develop a "can-do" attitude. Too often, we operate out of an "I don't think I can" attitude.

What a person thinks about is what he will manifest in his life. If you begin from the thought that it's hard to take the weight off, then that will be reality for you. You will never take the weight off because you believe it's just too hard.

We already know it's going to be hard, but is it really "too hard"? Nothing's too hard for us if we develop a can-do attitude. With a can-do attitude, we know the weight will come off. While we know it might not be easy—in fact it could be very hard—we also know it is possible as long as we go for it.

When we have an "I don't think I can" attitude, we may start the journey but will never be successful because we haven't switched to an "I can" mindset.

The battlefield is in the mind. What we're focused on becomes our reality. Don't view the ninety-one days as a finishing line but as a starting line.

As of right now, you're on the right track. The changes you've made should become part of an entire lifestyle, not part of a temporary sprint toward your goals with a backslide following.

I know that, for me, these ninety-one days have brought about huge change in my life, but it needs to remain a lasting change. If I choose to stop cultivating the new habits I have developed, the change in my life will be only temporary.

If we all could just make the switch from "I can't" to "I can," what a monumental difference that would make.

DAY 84
Can-Do Attitude

What have you told yourself in the past you couldn't do but now are telling yourself you can?

Learn

We need to get away from destructive behaviors and patterns. Our old behaviors and patterns got us were we were eighty-five days ago.

The only way to change our old, destructive behaviors and patterns is by inputting new information and then choosing to do something different—and then following through.

Information without action won't benefit us much. Action without information, on the other hand, will maybe move us closer to our goals, but without being properly informed, we may be taking the wrong actions and not realizing it.

We probably already know what foods are healthy and that we should exercise. But the more information we have on these subjects, the more effective we will become in attaining wellness. We can learn not just to eat healthily but also to turn our bodies into fat-burning machines.

When we educate ourselves and follow through with actions, nothing can hold us back. Continue to learn, continue to take action, and you will continue forward toward a new, better you!

More "What If"

What if life doesn't get any better? What if your health continues to deteriorate for the rest of your life? What if your marriage goes down the tubes? What if your career not only never gets better but continually gets worse? What if your weight continues to go up and never down? Will you be happy?

These are things that usually only happen if we let them. We have control in most areas of our life. We can let life knock us down, or we can live life on our terms. We can choose to be healthy and to drop the weight. We can be victorious in our careers. We can continue to learn and grow in our life. We can choose to make our marriage the best it's ever been. We all have the choice.

Making no choice is a choice. It's a choice to be complacent and to let life just happen. I don't think this is how you or I want to live.

We have a very short time here in this world. The time to act, the time to change to get your best life, is—NOW! Let's not waste another minute; let's live the best life we possibly can.

In not wasting another minute, you will be blessed in every avenue of your life.

What if you go back to your old ways after you complete day 91? What will that mean for you and your loved ones?

_____
_____
_____
_____
_____
_____
_____
_____
_____
_____
_____

Body by You

You get to design the body you want. We all get to pick—just as if we went to pick out a new outfit. We can choose an outfit that just hangs on us and doesn't look attractive, or we can choose one that fits well and makes us feel good and look good.

The outfit that fits well and looks good costs us in time, preparation, and sweat. It may cost more than a cheap one up front, but the end result is worth it. We will like the way we feel and look when we finally put on that new outfit.

It's the same with our bodies. Do we want ours to be unattractive and uncomfortable?

A healthy, attractive body costs us something, but so does an unhealthy, unattractive one. We pay with depression, lack of motivation, even overall unhappiness.

The healthy one might cost more at first in workout time, food preparation, sweat, and tears, but the end result will be rewarding. The reward outweighs the initial cost, just like with a high-quality piece of clothing.

An unhealthy body might seem like a better bargain at first, considering the cheaper foods it takes to get it and without the need to set aside time for exercising. But in the long haul, it will cost you the rest of your life by leaving you feeling unfulfilled, which is an expense none of us can afford.

Which outfit (body) do you choose to get and why?

_____
_____
_____
_____
_____
_____
_____
_____
_____
_____

The Power of 2

Ever heard of The Two-Horse Rule? Here it is: "The concept of teamwork can be illustrated by the two-horse rule. If one horse can pull 700 pounds, and another horse can pull 800 pounds, how much weight will they pull yoked together? The two-horse team will pull their own weight plus the weight of their partner. Therefore, yoked together, the horses can pull 3,000 pounds!"

Finding someone else who shares our goals can be very motivating. I think this is why people lose weight on *The Biggest Loser* who just couldn't seem to do it alone.

There really is strength in numbers. Contestants on the show have teammates who encourage one another. They also have a trainer to motivate them, a doctor to track their progress and show them how much healthier they are becoming along the way, and a nutritionist to teach them how to make minor food swaps for healthier dishes. With the power of more than one, they set themselves up for success.

You and a workout buddy can motivate each other. A trainer can also help push us out of our comfort zone. And if you can get your family on board with healthier meals, the odds of making a successful lifestyle change will dramatically increase.

To this point, you may have been succeeding on your own, and that's great. But there can be great power in being united with someone who shares your goal.

Think of someone you can get on board with you, and you both win!

DAY 88
The Power of 2

Who could you incorporate into your life to draw from the power of 2?

Self-Talk (Part 3)

On days 62 and 63, we talked about the importance of self-talk. I challenged you to print or write out Zig Ziglar's self-talk cards and read them out loud every morning as soon as you got up and every evening before you went to bed. So how did you do?

Now, you don't have to use Zig's self-talk cards exclusively. You can create your own and use them if you choose. That's what I have done. You can use either mine or Zig's as a template to develop your own. Following are my self-talk cards that I have developed for myself.

I (Your Name) am a child of God created in His image and likeness.

I (Your Name) am the salt of the earth and the light of the world. God knew perfectly well what He was doing when He made me, and since He doesn't make mistakes, there's no junk in me. He guides my footsteps and has endowed me with integrity, kindness, and strength. He has given me the ability to learn and grow and to love others—to not be self-seeking but to always see opportunities to help others. He has blessed me with a wife above all others, therefore I will seek to bring her joy and show her that she is loved each and every day.

I (Your Name) treat my business as a business and instinctively know how to grow it and will have the energy and strength to follow through.

I (Your Name) will work on relationships with family and friends to build everlasting bonds. I was born to win, and any temporary setback or failure is only an event and not me as a person. I take pride in my appearance and my abilities and am excited about my future and what life has to offer me. Today is going to be great, and I will live it to the fullest!

The Results

Today is result day. Unfortunately, I took no measurements, no body-fat percentage or anything of the sort to guide me in my assessment. The only measuring tool I used was the scale itself.

On day 1, I weighed in at 256 pounds, just four pounds down from my heaviest. This week I weighed in at 230 pounds—a twenty-six pound weight loss in ninety days. Not too bad. That's a healthy weight loss of about two pounds every week.

But the biggest accomplishments weren't seen on the scale. In the past 90 days, I increased my sales at work around 30 percent more than any previous quarter that I have had in about ten years.

I'm also happier and enjoy life more than ever. I've become a positive influence on family and friends. My marriage is getting stronger.

I gained the energy to run a half marathon in the last ninety days, too. My clothes fit better, and I feel better.

I completed this book by writing a page every day for the past ninety days. In the past, this is the kind of project I would have started but would have never seen it through to completion. Now I'm resolved to follow through on my ideas.

I also took a day-long and a two-day-long sales-essentials class to better myself. I would have considered doing something like this in the past but probably would have never spent the money on the classes themselves (plus the airfare and hotel). I'm not wishing or hoping to do something anymore—today I'm doing it!

The scale is just the byproduct of learning to live my life differently. When the inside changes, the outside changes, too. That's what this journey has been all about for us: building a new better you from the inside out!

DAY 90

The Results

What results have you seen in the last ninety days?

A New Beginning

As we come to the end of our journey together, don't let this be the end of change in your life but rather a new beginning. You are well on your way to accomplishing everything you want in life. Keep your chin up, and keep pressing forward.

I want to thank you for the opportunity to allow me to be a coach, motivator, and something of a mentor in your life for the last ninety-one days. Use this book often: a second reading will help you grow even more, and if I was able to help you in your journey, then please don't forget to pass this book on to others who could also benefit from it. We succeed when we help others succeed.

Be proud of yourself, live with passion, and may God be with you!

Acknowledgments

This book was made possible only by the love and support of my wife, Kathy. She inspires me with the love and joy that she shows to others, and I'm grateful for her love and support that she shows me daily. I would like to also acknowledge the Ziglar Corporation for keeping the message of Zig Ziglar alive. I am grateful also for the positive influences from the teachings of Jaret Grossman. Last but not least, I would like to thank the God of Abraham, Isaac, and Jacob as I feel His hand helped guide me through the writing process, and I dedicate the writing of this book to the uplifting of His name.

About the Author

Joseph Abney is a man of integrity and faith. Joseph has been a high-performance salesman for more than twenty years. He has taught hundreds of people the art of sales and has had a passion for self-improvement throughout his sales career. Joseph applies that same zeal to his desire to know and teach biblical principles. Joseph has done an amazing job of transferring his knowledge, abilities, and life experiences from his career and spiritual life to the area of health. He has a gift of encouraging and teaching others to see their health goals through and to stop giving up on themselves. His mentoring brings a happiness and self-confidence that can be applied to all areas of your life.

www.ingramcontent.com/pod-product-compliance
Lightning Source LLC
Chambersburg PA
CBHW071153300426
44113CB00009B/1194